John Hardwick works under the banner of *Counties* and *Children W*
Christian message in an exciting way, which will appeal to people
received in schools, churches and at outreach events, John works witl
all ages and backgrounds. His skills in clowning, juggling, unicycling, s
a proven success. John leads *Creative Communications* training eve......
children's ministry and all-age services, where his workshops include key areas such as
storytelling and presenting the Bible through music. He also organizes sessions for worship
leaders, family and all-age services and holiday clubs. John is a familiar face at Spring Harvest,
Easter People and other Christian events, where he leads family and children's sessions. John
is a member of the *Barnabas* freelance team and author of *Barnabas'* ever-popular holiday
club resources, *We're going on a Jungle Jamboree*, *Champions!*, *Junior Heroes!* and *Starship
Discovery!*

Important information

Photocopying permission

The right to photocopy material in *Razzamatazz Robots Holiday Club!* is granted for
the pages that contain the photocopying clause, 'Reproduced with permission from
Razzamatazz Robots Holiday Club! published by BRF 2009, ISBN 978 1 84101 577 4', so long
as reproduction is for use in a teaching situation by the original purchaser. The right to
photocopy material is not granted for anyone other than the original purchaser without
written permission from BRF.

The Copyright Licensing Agency (CLA)

If you are resident in the UK and you have a photocopying licence with the Copyright Licensing
Agency (CLA), please check the terms of your licence. If your photocopying request falls within
the terms of your licence, you may proceed without seeking further permission. If your
request exceeds the terms of your CLA licence, please contact the CLA direct with your
request. Copyright Licensing Agency, 90 Tottenham Court Road, London W1T 4LP. Telephone
020 7631 5555; fax 020 7631 5500; email cla@cla.co.uk; website www.cla.co.uk. The CLA will
provide photocopying authorization and royalty fee information on behalf of BRF.

BRF is a Registered Charity (No. 233280)

Text copyright © John Hardwick 2009
Illustrations copyright © Simon Smith 2009
The author asserts the moral right
to be identified as the author of this work

Published by
The Bible Reading Fellowship
15 The Chambers, Vineyard
Abingdon OX14 3FE
United Kingdom
Tel: +44 (0)1865 319700
Email: enquiries@brf.org.uk
Website: www.brf.org.uk

ISBN 978 1 84101 577 4
First published 2009
10 9 8 7 6 5 4 3 2 1 0
All rights reserved

Acknowledgments
Scripture quotations taken from the Holy Bible, New International Version, copyright © 1973, 1978, 1984 by International
Bible Society, are used by permission of Hodder & Stoughton Publishers, a division of Hodder Headline Ltd. All rights reserved.
'NIV' is a registered trademark of International Bible Society. UK trademark number 1448790.

Scriptures quoted from the Good News Bible published by The Bible Societies/HarperCollins Publishers Ltd, UK © American
Bible Society 1966, 1971, 1976, 1992, used with permission.

Performance and copyright
The right to perform *Razzamatazz Robots Holiday Club* drama material is included in the purchase price, so long as the
performance is in an amateur context, for instance in church services, schools or holiday club venues. Where any charge is
made to audiences, written permission must be obtained from the author, who can be contacted through the publishers.
A fee or royalties may be payable for the right to perform the script in that context.

A catalogue record for this book is available from the British Library

Printed in Singapore by Craft Print International Ltd

Razzamatazz Robots Holiday Club!

A five-day holiday club plan, complete and ready-to-run

John Hardwick

This book is dedicated to my father, Leslie Hardwick, and my late mother, Ruth, who were involved in reaching out to children through Skegness beach missions, camps and regular Sunday school and midweek children's clubs. They have helped me to see the importance of reaching children with the good news of God's love.

Acknowledgments

With thanks to the following people for their help and inspiration:
My wife, Rachel, and children, Chloe and Ben.
Sue Doggett, my ever-patient editor.
Simon Smith, for his fantastic artwork.
With many thanks to David Wilkinson for the sheet music notation on pages 14–21.
Thanks also to St John's Parish Church ,Woodbridge, Suffolk and Detling Conference for allowing me to try out my new theme on them and for helping with ideas.

Contents

Foreword

Several months ago, my mum sorted through some of my late gran's old stuff. It had been stored in the attic of a house that my brother intended to renovate, and it needed to be sold or thrown out or distributed among my siblings and nieces and nephews. One of the things she found was a cardboard box. It didn't look like much on the outside, and to the untrained eye its contents didn't seem to be very valuable, either. But as soon as she opened it my hand shot up and my mouth shouted, 'Mine!'

You see, I had made some of the things in that box—or, to be entirely honest, I had helped my grandmother make those things—in preparation for a Holiday Bible Club she'd led when I was just nine or ten. There were picture frames and pencil holders and table mats, made mostly from frozen lolly sticks—the default craft material of the 1960s!

I loved making those things with my gran. I loved Holiday Bible Club, as well—the games, the songs, the stories, the lot. And that's one of the reasons I like this book. Good Holiday Bible Club teaching material makes for good Holiday Bible Clubs, and good Holiday Bible Clubs make good memories—memories that can last a lifetime.

The second reason I like this book is that it was written by John Hardwick. I've known John for several years now and worked with him on many occasions. I've listened to his stories and sung his songs and tried to keep up with his actions and marvelled at his energy. You can hear John as you read this book—and that's a good thing. His enthusiasm and humour and dedication to presenting God's word in a way that kids can enjoy and understand jumps right off these pages. Just like John jumps!

That brings me to the third reason. Kids really need to hear the message in this book. When I go to schools, one of the stories I make sure the children hear is the creation story, and that's because they need to know that they are not in this world by mistake or by accident. They need to know that 'someone' made them, and that that 'someone' made them unique and special—not robots; not clones; not objects to be discarded when the batteries run out. The other thing they need to know is that that 'someone' made the person sitting next to them, as well, and that that person is just as special, just as unique and just as precious—not a robot, either. The two things together make community possible. John has done a wonderful job of tracing the story of God's plan to recreate that community, once it had been lost, through his steadfast love.

God made a good world. John made a good book about it. I think you'll find it really useful. And you know the best thing of all? He didn't need to use even one frozen lolly stick. My gran would have been impressed.

Bob Hartman

Introduction

Robots are here to stay! With the return of K9, the launch of the BBC's interactive *Little Robots*, films such as *Wall.e*, about the little robot who cleans up planet earth, robot kits and *Robots* the DVD, there is no doubt that robots are very popular. Robots are carefully designed—every little detail plays its part—but, however clever and amazing robots are, they will never be alive in the way we are. When God created human beings he made us in his image. He gave us the ability to work things out and be creative, to communicate and make choices. Robots may have adventures in the world of film and television, they may fight wars on the silver screen and delight small children with their quirky 'characters', but they are controlled and limited in what they can do and they will never be human.

Overview

The Razzamatazz Robots Holiday Club! is a fun-filled adventure, designed to help children understand the important truth of God's plan for each one of us. With plenty of opportunities for recreation along the way, the five sessions unpack the plan of the Master Designer from creation to re-creation as follows:

Day One: Creation appreciation!

The story of creation in Genesis shows us just how wonderfully designed and beautiful our world is. First of all, light started shining and God created day and night. Next he created water below and above the surface of the earth and formed the land and the sea. Then he made green growing things, followed by the sun, moon and stars; then fish, birds and animals all bursting forth at the command of the Master Creator. The genesis of creation is a pastiche of colour, taste and smell, tactile and full of sound—a tapestry of unity within diversity. God looked at what he had done, and it was good.

- Bible story: Genesis 1:1–25
- Memory verse: 'God saw all that he had made and it was very good! God saw all that he had made and he was well pleased, well pleased!' (Based on Genesis 1:31, GNB)

Day Two: Creation's crown!

Finally, God made human beings—the crown of his creation. He did not create us to roll off a robotic production line; he created us to be like him—able to think and feel, to be creative and to make choices. He made each one of us in his own image, but each one of us is special and unique: he created us with diversity within unity. He created our bodies with intricate detail, each part having its own special role to play. He made our minds to think creatively and our spirits to walk with him.

- Bible story: Genesis 1:26–31; 2:4b–25; Psalm 8:5
- Memory verse: 'I praise you because I am fearfully and wonderfully made; your works are wonderful, I know that full well' (Psalm 139:14, NIV).

Day Three: Careless whispers!

The ability to make choices means that we can get things right—or wrong. And it wasn't long before Adam and Eve started to get things very wrong. Walking in God's gorgeous garden one day, a thought popped into Eve's head that made her doubt everything she had, until then, believed to be true. The story tells of a cunning snake, whispering in her ear, 'What about that tree in the middle of the garden? Why shouldn't you be able to eat the delicious fruit hanging so temptingly from its branches?' Should she or shouldn't she? Poor Eve, she made the wrong choice! God didn't make us like robots, unable to make our own decisions. He made us with independent minds because he wanted us to be his friends, not his automata. And so creation's caretakers became creation's takers. No longer able to be trusted, we were banished from God's perfect garden.

- Bible story: Genesis 3:1–8
- Memory verse: 'Remember the Lord in all things, and he will show you the right way to go' (Based on Proverbs 3:6, GNB).

Day Four: Enough's enough!

Before long, people were living in every corner of the earth, but things went from bad to worse. Everything they thought and planned was evil. God was very, very sad. His beautiful creation was being spoilt by the selfishness and greed of the very people who were meant to look after it. Only one person, Noah, seemed to be making the right choice and following the Lord. Enough was enough! God decided to start again. He kept Noah and his family safe, but everyone else was washed away in a great flood. Noah was saved because of his great love for God and because he chose what was right. When the flood was over, Noah and his family and all the animals stepped on to the rainwashed soil of a new beginning. Then God set a rainbow in the sky as a sign of his promise never to destroy the world again.

- Bible story: Genesis 6:1—9:17
- Memory verse: 'Love the Lord your God with all your heart, with all your soul, with all your strength, and with all your mind, and love your neighbour as you love yourself' (Luke 10:27, GNB).

Day Five: The Master's plan

Not being a robot is great, but there is just one big snag: however hard we try, we keep getting things wrong. We just can't help ourselves. God has given us the Master Designer's instruction book to show us the right way. The trouble is, often we don't read it and, when we do, we still get things wrong. The Bible is full of stories about how people made the wrong choice and how God tried to help them get it right. But sending a message secondhand isn't always the best way to get us to listen. So God put his master plan into place and came himself to show us the way to live.

- Bible story: Luke 2:1–7; John 1:1–5, 14; Mark 1:1–11; Colossians 1:15–20
- Memory verse: 'Jesus said, "I am the way, the truth and the life; no one comes to the Father except through me!"' (Based on John 14:6, NIV)

Extra story

God's love goes on and on and on! Ideal for a Sunday service or special holiday club event, this Bible story tells how God never gives up on us. Even when we wander off and lose our way, he doesn't forget us. He comes looking for us as if we were the only person in the world and, when he finds us, he gently leads us back into the fold of his love and throws a party in heaven to celebrate. What a great God!

- Bible story: Luke 15:4–6
- Memory verse: 'For God so loved the world, he gave his only Son. And whoever believes in him shall not die but have eternal life' (Based on John 3:16, NIV).

Setting up

To set the scene for your holiday club, you could decorate the room with a mixture of different focal areas. One area could focus on 'God the Creator', showing the universe and space, pictures and models of trees, animals, people and other aspects of God's creation. Another area could focus on things that human beings have invented, such as cars, aeroplanes and plenty of robots. A third area could include a display about the environment and ways in which we can help to look after our wonderful planet.

Use the internet to find pictures and images for each area. You should be able to find some of the popular robots featured in films and television programmes for children by keying their names into a search engine. You could build some of the robot images into a rolling PowerPoint presentation for the children to enjoy as they arrive. They will no doubt recognize some of the popular robot characters.

Roles and responsibilities

Good teamwork is essential for good children's work. As well as an overall holiday club coordinator, you'll need people to fill all the following roles.

Registration officer

This role would suit a well-organized person. If the children are registered before the start date of the holiday club, you will save time on the first day of the club. If you choose to register the children on the first day, you will need a good team of helpers to cope with the workload.

You need to register the following details for each child.

- Name and address
- Date of birth
- Contact phone number
- Medical details (such as asthma or allergies)
- Parent's or guardian's permission for child to attend the club

You will need to split children into groups according to their age bands, and possibly sub-section them into teams. It's advisable to issue each child with a colour-coded sticker or badge to identify him or her and the team to which they belong. Have a 'welcome' team available 15 minutes before the start to make the children feel at home when they arrive.

Team leaders

Team leaders need to be able to deal with a high level of responsibility. Each team leader will be allocated to a particular group of children or age band. They will stay with the children the whole time, sitting with them and leading them through various activities. They will befriend, enthuse and maintain a level of control. It's important that team leaders join in the songs, as children will look to their leaders as role models.

Team helpers

These are people who can help the team leader. They need to be free to fetch things, accompany children to the toilet and so on.

Games leader

This needs to be someone with experience of sorting children quickly, and accustomed to organizing games. A powerful voice would be an asset. Keep the games in one location and bring the children to that area when it is their turn to play.

Craft leader

This needs to be someone able to organize a simple craft activity. The craft leader will need to start collecting materials well in advance. Try to make the crafts theme-related. Once again, have a fixed location for crafts and bring the children to that area when it is their turn.

Time keeper

This person watches the time and gives a five-minute warning to activity leaders that the session is about to end. He or she then rings a bell when it's time for the teams to move on to the next activity.

Snack team

One person or team is needed to prepare drinks and biscuits for the children. Not all the children will need their drinks at the same time, as teams will take turns to have their refreshments. Please ensure that all the leaders, including the game leader and craft leader, also receive drinks.

First aider

It is essential to have someone available who is a trained first aider, and to have a well-stocked first aid box. St John Ambulance may be able to offer advice if you are unsure about how to provide this facility.

Discipler

Children may have questions about the Christian faith. Disciplers need to be able to talk in simple language and be good listeners. They should know what they believe and how to put it across without manipulation or forcing the children into making statements or promises they cannot understand or keep.

You will need to think about how to follow up children who are seeking to know more about the Christian faith.

Publicity officer

This person is needed to design and organize posters, leaflets and school visits, and to contact the local press.

Floaters

Floaters are helpers who cannot commit themselves to the whole week's programme but are able to come for a day or two. They can help wherever there is a need.

Stage team or presenter

Either one person or a team is needed to lead the up-front programme, leading the songs, theme illustration, quiz, Bible story and teaching, and introducing the drama and puppet sketches. You may wish to fill this role from your own team, or you may decide to give your regular children's leaders a rest and bring in someone from outside.

Dos and don'ts

It's worth repeating that good children's work relies on good teamwork!

- Do sit with the children during up-front time.
- Do be prepared to join in the songs and interactive parts of the programme. Don't forget that children will look to the team leaders as their role models.
- Do encourage, befriend and control your team of children.
- Do use your common sense.
- Do encourage children to go to the toilet during the activity times rather than the up-front/teaching times. Remember that children follow each other's lead: if you're not careful, all the young ones will decide at once that they need an outing to the toilet.
- Do expect to have fun yourself and be open to learn. The teaching aspect of the programme is not just for the kids—God may choose to speak to you, too.
- Don't loiter on the edge, chatting or distracting the children or presenter, as the programme is taking place.

concerning the Safeguarding Vulnerable Groups Act 2006, such as *Every Child Matters* (DfES) and *Safe from Harm* (Home Office 1993).

- No team member should be alone with a child where their activity cannot be seen by others.
- Always treat the children with respect and dignity.
- Never use physical punishment.
- Ensure that more than one person is present if a child needs to be washed or helped in the toilet.
- Male team members should not accompany female children to the toilet.
- Do not become overfriendly, with children sitting on your lap, hugging, or rough-and-tumbling.
- Do not play-fight with children or join in games where you could fall on a child.
- Do not run around with children on your shoulders.
- Do not go into a room alone with a child and never arrange to meet a child alone.
- Avoid any inappropriate touching or any excessively rough or physical games.
- Do not engage in any scapegoating, ridiculing or rejection of a child.
- Do not invite a child to your home alone.
- Avoid giving lifts to children on their own. If a car journey is necessary, a second person should be present and the child should sit on a rear seat of the car, using an appropriate seat belt.
- If you need to contact a child at home during or after the holiday club, ensure that you identify yourself as a member of the holiday club team.
- If abuse is suspected, do not encourage the child to talk further. Report suspicions immediately to the holiday club coordinator and make written notes of anything you and the child said to each other.

Fire safety

- Do not use candles, matches or lighters on the premises.
- Familiarize yourself with the fire exits.
- Observe fire drills: they are for everybody's safety.

Safety first

 Child protection guidelines should be observed at all times, in order to maintain the safety and well-being of the children and members of the team. Any questions relating to Criminal Records Bureau (CRB) checks and disclosure should be raised with your church council, diocese or denominational body well before your holiday club start date. The points below are for general guidance only and are not intended to replace official documents

Stay legal

- If your holiday club lasts for more than two hours and runs for six days or more in a year, you need to register with Social Services. If you are planning follow-up events, this rule might affect you.
- If under-8s are involved, write to inform Social Services of your plans.
- Have someone on security to stop children from wandering out or strangers from wandering into your premises.

For further information about legal requirements for child protection, contact your local council, your diocese or church office, or:

The Criminal Records Bureau
CRB Customer Services
PO Box 110, Liverpool L69 3EF
Tel: 0870 9090811
Website: www.crb.gov.uk

The Churches Child Protection Advisory Service
Disclosure Service
PO Box 133, Swanley, Kent BR8 7UQ
Telephone: 0845 120 4549
Fax: 0845 120 4552
E-mail: disclosure@ccpas.co.uk
Website: www.ccpas.co.uk

Incentives

Throughout our lives, we have incentives to help us achieve our very best, and to keep up our enthusiasm and excitement for the job in hand. In schools, children are awarded stars or house points and receive qualifications, which reflect their achievements. In the workplace, there are company perks, plus the chance of promotion or a pay rise. Incentives can help with the boredom of routine. There is always a new target to reach.

At weekly children's clubs, incentives or a little competition can help to create and maintain enthusiasm, and there are many ways you can add them to the weekly programme. For example, with a personal achievement chart or a team achievement score board, children can earn points that are visible on a card, scoring chart or token. They earn points for:

• Attendance
• Answering a question in the quiz
• Being the coolest-behaved girl and boy
• Being outstanding at joining in activities
• Bringing along a friend

The scoring chart could be based on the theme of the day. For example:

• **Creation appreciation**: Have a team tree, or give each child their own tree to 'climb'. Stickers are added to the tree as the children progress.
• **Creation's crown**: Make a team crown out of gold card, or give each child a small card crown. Stickers are added to decorate the crown for each point won.
• **Careless whispers**: Make a slithery snake out of card for each team, or give each child a slithery snake card. Stickers are added to create a pattern on the snake's back for each point won.

• **Enough's enough**: Cut a simple ark shape out of card for each team, or give each child a small ark-shaped card. Have a pack of animal-shaped stickers to add to the ark as each point is won.
• **The Master's plan**: Make a simple hand shape for each team, or give each child his or her own hand shape to which stickers are added. When a child reaches five stickers, he or she receives a small prize (for example, a sweet). When the child reaches ten stickers, he or she is given a bigger prize (for example, an item such as a pencil, yo-yo or badge).

You could continue the incentive by having a big prizegiving event at the end of the holiday club to which parents are invited. If you choose to do this, make sure you keep it light-hearted and have something for everyone, so that individual children don't feel that they are missing out.

Equally, you could have a different chart or card for each day, or use tokens instead. If tokens are used, a child receives a token for the same reasons as before, which can be exchanged at the end of the day for a prize.

Try to avoid the 'tuck shop' idea where children can exchange their own money for sweets. Some children have plenty of money, while others have very little. It's far better to have a prize system where they all have an equal opportunity to earn a prize.

Prayer

Many children who come along to holiday clubs may never have had the opportunity to pray at home or school, so they may not realize that God actually wants them to pray to him. You may wish to consider using the holiday club to introduce children to prayer, encouraging them to pray in a simple way. It is helpful to remind the children about who God is and to explain that, even though he is so great, he still wants us to talk to him. Talking to God is called prayer. We can pray to God at any time and about anything. God listens to every word. We don't just ask God for lots of different things for ourselves —that would be greedy. We ask him to help others, especially our friends and family.

Include a few sample prayers to help the children get started. For example, as the Razzamatazz Robots theme is about the celebration of life, the prayer might be, 'Thank you, God, for giving me my life. Help me to live it for you!'

There are some creative prayer suggestions on pages 86 and 92.

Daily programmes

Day One: Creation appreciation!

The story of creation in Genesis shows us just how wonderfully designed and beautiful our world is. The genesis of creation is a pastiche of colour, taste and smell, tactile and full of sound— a tapestry of unity within diversity. God looked at what he had done and it was good.

Bible story: Genesis 1:1–25
Memory verse: God saw all that he had made and it was very good! God saw all that he had made and he was well pleased, well pleased! (based on Genesis 1:31, GNB).

Day Two: Creation's crown!

Finally, God made human beings—the crown of his creation. He did not create us to roll off a robotic production line; he created us to be like him—able to think and feel, to be creative and to make choices. He made each one of us in his own image, but each one of us is special and unique: he created us with diversity within unity.

Bible story: Genesis 1:26–31; 2:4b–25; Psalm 8:5
Memory verse: I praise you because I am fearfully and wonderfully made; your works are wonderful, I know that full well (Psalm 139:14, NIV).

I will praise you because of the wonderful way you created me

Day Three: Careless whispers!

The ability to make choices means that we can get things right—or wrong. And it wasn't long before Adam and Eve started to get things very wrong. As they were no longer able to be trusted, the story recounts how they were banished from God's perfect garden.

Bible story: Genesis 3:1–8
Memory verse: Remember the Lord in all things, and he will show you the right way to go (based on Proverbs 3:6, GNB).

Day Four: Enough's enough!

God kept Noah and his family safe because Noah loved God and chose what was right. After the flood, God set a rainbow in the sky as a sign of his promise never to destroy the world again.

Bible story: Genesis 6:1—9:17
Memory verse: Love the Lord your God with all your heart, with all your soul, with all your strength, and with all your mind, and love your neighbour as you love yourself (Luke 10:27, GNB).

Day Five: The Master's plan

Not being a robot is great, but there is just one big snag: however hard we try, we keep getting things wrong. We just can't help ourselves. So God put his master plan into action and came himself to show us the way to live.

Bible story: Luke 2:1–7; John 1:1–5, 14; Mark 1:1–11; Colossians 1:15–20
Memory verse: Jesus said, 'I am the way, the truth and the life; no one comes to the Father except through me!' (Based on John 14:6, NIV).

Extra story

God's love goes on and on and on! Even when we wander off and lose our way, he doesn't forget us. He comes looking for us and, when he finds us, he gently leads us back into the fold of his love and throws a party in heaven to celebrate. What a great God!

Bible story: Luke 15:4–6
Memory verse: For God so loved the world, he gave his only Son. And whoever believes in him shall not die but have eternal life (John 3:16, NIV)

Razzamatazz Robots! timetable

A two-and-a-half-hour programme (adaptable to suit your situation)

9.15am: Team meet together to pray.

9.35am: Last-minute preparation.

9.45am: Doors open for registration. Split the children into three teams according to their ages. Children go to team leaders/areas.

10.00am: Stage-based presentation/up-front time 1 (30 minutes):
- Introduction and welcome
- Opening talk to introduce the theme for the day
- Theme song (see page 14 for details)
- Action song
- Theme illustration or theme team challenge
- Memory verse song
- Watt family daily drama
- Song or Bible memory verse recap

10.30am: Activity time: three activities, each lasting for 25 minutes. In their teams, the children rotate round the different activities so that all the children do each activity:
- Game
- Craft
- Snack, chat and funsheet

12.00pm: Stage-based presentation/up-front time 2 (30 minutes).
- Songs
- Puppet sketch
- Bible memory verse recap
- Quick quiz
- Bible story
- Round-up/prayer
- Theme song

12.30pm: Children go back to small groups and wait to be collected.

Razzamatazz Robots! theme song

'Razzamatazz' means flamboyant bustle or activity, so create that razzle-dazzle atmosphere with the following song.

The Watt Family theme song

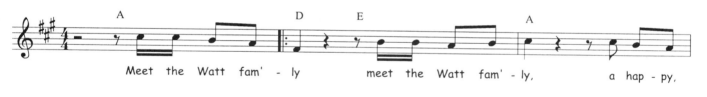

Meet the Watt fam' - ly   meet the Watt fam' - ly,   a hap - py,

wack - y, cra - zy, ord - in - ar - y fam - i - ly.   Meet the Watt fam' - ly,   meet the Watt fam' -

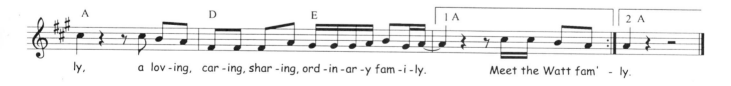

ly,   a lov - ing, car - ing, shar - ing, ord - in - ar - y fam - i - ly.   Meet the Watt fam' - ly.

Razzamatazz Robots! Bible memory verse songs

The Bible memory verses are based on the text of either the NIV or the Good News Bible. However, they do not necessarily include the whole verse, and the wording may vary slightly to fit the melody.

All the songs that accompany the *Razzamatazz Robots* holiday club programme can be downloaded from John Hardwick's website: www.johnhardwick.org.uk. Please remember to include all songs on your church's CCL (Christian Copyright Licence) Song Survey Worksheet.

Day One: Creation appreciation

It was good!

I will praise you

Remember, remember

Love the Lord your God

Who said, 'I'm the way'?

John four-teen, verse six. John four-teen, verse six. John four-teen, verse six.

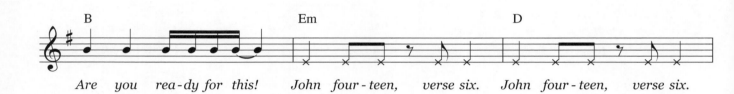

Are you rea-dy for this! John four-teen, verse six. John four-teen, verse six.

John four-teen, verse six. Are you rea-dy for this! Who said, 'I'm the way'?

Je-sus said, 'I'm the way'. Who said, 'I'm the truth'?___ Je-sus said, 'I'm the truth'.

Who said, 'I'm the life'? Je-sus said, 'I'm the life'._ With-out me!

No one can go___ to the Fa - ther!

For God so loved the world

Razzamatazz rap

The verses are sung in the style of a chant, with the leader singing a line and everybody else echoing what was sung—in the way that the American army sings as the soldiers jog along.

Yeah, yeah *(echo)*, listen to me *(echo)*.
It's the Master's plan *(echo)* that will set you free *(echo)*.

Jesus came to show the way
Of the Master's plan for us today.
We're not robots, we have the choice
To turn away or follow God's voice!

Yeah, yeah *(echo)*, listen to me *(echo)*.
It's the Master's plan *(echo)* that will set you free*(echo)*.

Jesus died, the price to pay,
But he rose again on Easter Day.
He opens the door and welcomes us in.
He died for us and forgave our sin.

Yeah, yeah *(echo)*, listen to me *(echo)*.
It's the Master's plan *(echo)* that will set you free *(echo)*.

Now God invites you and me
To be a part of his great family!
The Master's plan for us will be
Final destination: heaven's party!

Yeah, yeah *(echo)*, listen to me *(echo)*.
It's the Master's plan *(echo)* that will set you free *(echo)*.

Copyright © John Hardwick (www.johnhardwick.org.uk)

Opening talks

Day One: Creation appreciation!

Start by giving an overall welcome to the *Razzamatazz Robots* holiday club. Then say, 'I wonder if we have got any robots here today? Are you sure? Look at the person next to you. Are they a human being or a robot? Look into their eyes, look at their nose and their hands. Thank goodness for that! Of course, everyone here is human.

'Don't worry, in real life you can't mistake a robot for a human being. Robots don't really look like humans. But perhaps you have seen the programme *Little Robots* on TV, or the films *Robots* or *Wall.e*, the little robot who cleans up planet earth? Or perhaps you have heard of iRobots? In films and on TV, some robots seem almost human, but real robots aren't like us—they can never be alive in the way that we are.'

Make it visual

Beforehand, make a junk robot out of small cardboard boxes, with yogurt pot eyes and so on. Show it to the children to illustrate the following story.

Say, 'Look what I've got here! Wow, you won't believe what happened this morning! I came downstairs and there in the middle of the living room was this robot *(show robot)*. I checked to see if my… *(name people you share a home with)* had made it, but none of them had. The only explanation is that the cardboard boxes and yogurt pots must have dragged themselves across the floor and all the bits just came together and made a robot. Isn't that amazing?

'Do you believe me? Of course you don't! We know *someone* made this robot. It couldn't just happen—it's been carefully designed and put together.'

Go on to explain that planet earth is amazing and, guess what? It was carefully designed and created by a master creator. *(Show a picture of planet earth.)*

Toy robot

Show a picture, or have to hand one of the amazing toy robots that are now available in toy shops. Show the picture or the toy robot to the children to illustrate the following thought.

Say, 'Just imagine what it would be like to meet the person who invented the amazing toy robots that you can buy nowadays. Imagine what it would be like if they tried to explain how they made the robot. Their explanation would probably be so complicated that we wouldn't understand a word they were saying. *(Show the picture of planet earth again.)*

'God made our wonderful, amazing and complex world. It's far cleverer than any robot. The Bible doesn't tell us *how* God made the world—the explanation would be very complicated. Instead, the Bible tells us a great story to help us understand *why* God made the world. We'll hear this wonderful story later.'

Day Two: Creation's crown!

Say, 'Which are better: robots or human beings? Robots can do jobs humans can't do! Robots never get distracted or bored or even tired. Provided they have a power supply, they can work 24/7. Robots can work without air, which is why they've already gone to Mars. Robots never argue.

'Well, it sounds as if robots are better than human beings! But are they really? Can you have a chat with a robot? Can you share a joke with a robot?

'The word "robot" actually means "slave", which in turn means forced labour. God didn't want a world full of mindless slaves or robots that he could control; he wanted the crown of his creation to be thinking and feeling human beings, with the capacity for loving, laughing and enjoying life.

'Human beings can think for themselves. Human beings can be great friends and are good at chatting. Human beings are creative and fun-loving. In fact, we humans are the crown of God's creation. We have the ability to think things through and work things out. We are the most amazing part of God's creation and, what's more, we've been made in his image. Wow!

'You and I are unique and amazing... what are we? Amazing! Some animals are clever, some are fantastic, but no animal has our imagination and creativity. No animal has ever invented so much as the wheel. Today we are going to discover more about how God made us and the purpose he has for our lives.'

Day Three: Careless whispers!

Adapt the following idea to suit your situation.

Say, 'I have two children and I love them very, very much. But there are times when I wish they were robots so that I could program them to obey instant commands, or so that I could just flick a switch for instant results. Wouldn't it be great to have a "tidy your room" switch, a "clean your teeth" switch, or an "increase speed" switch?

'It would be so useful, especially in the morning when their mum and I are trying to get them out to school. They get distracted so easily! I'm constantly asking, "Are you out of bed yet? Are you dressed yet? Are you downstairs yet? Have you cleaned your teeth yet?" Does that sound familiar? Is it like that in your house, too? Oh, how I wish I could just flick a switch so that they would do these things instantly.

'But we're not machines or robots. We're people with personalities and that's exactly how God wants us to be. The only problem is that this means we're not perfect and sometimes (in fact, quite often) we get things wrong and make mistakes.

'Later, we're going to hear about a big mistake that spoilt everything.'

Day Four: Enough's enough!

Say, 'Yesterday we thought about how wonderful it would be to have children with switches built in, to be able to make them do things instantly, such as a "tidy your room" switch, a "clean your teeth" switch, or an "increase speed" switch. We also thought about how sometimes we make mistakes and let each other down.

'But just imagine how horrible it is for a mum or dad when their child deliberately and constantly disobeys them all the time. Mums and dads would soon become very sad if that happened, and everyone's life would be miserable because of the child's behaviour.

'Perhaps a mum or dad in that situation really might start to wish that their son or daughter were just a robot, instead of a human being with the ability to choose to do wrong things all the time. How very sad! The Bible tells us that, unfortunately, human beings started to behave like that right from the beginning of time. They constantly and deliberately disobeyed God until, finally, God had to say, "Enough is enough."'

Day Five: The Master's plan

Say, 'Have you noticed how some people seem to love their car or their computer more than they love actual people? But however much attention someone pays to a car or a computer, they certainly don't very often give it a hug! We all rely on gadgets at home, such as a washing machine or a vacuum cleaner, and they rarely let us down, but most of us don't love these things more than we love people.

'In the future, everyone's home may be filled with robots to do the household chores, and I'm sure that people will think their robots are wonderful, but even highly sophisticated robots will never be able to replace a living person in terms of love and affection.

'Children and parents sometimes let each other down, but above all they love each other. Even when we've done something wrong, we show each other affection. Perhaps you have seen a mum or dad give their little child a hug just as he or she is lining up to go into their classroom at school. Perhaps this has happened to you.

'When we show affection to each other, it makes us feel loved and valued. After the flood had subsided and Noah was ready to leave the ark, if I had been God I would probably have said to Noah and his family, "Before you go off into the world, I just want to put a control panel in your head so that I can flick a switch and stop you doing bad things. Is that OK?" God didn't choose to do that, but he did have a plan! He knew that, because he had given us the capacity to make choices, we would sometimes make wrong choices and get ourselves into a mess. But, because God loves us very much, he will always forgive us if we accept and follow his plan. God wants us to choose to be his friend for eternity.'

Theme illustrations and team challenges

Children love being volunteers, so here is an opportunity for them to be involved, have fun and learn something all at the same time. For each day, you have the choice of either a theme illustration or a team challenge: choose the one to suit your club. **NB:** These activities work better if the volunteers are older children.

If you choose to have a team challenge, be aware that they can absorb a lot of your up-front time, so keep them tightly controlled. You may wish to prime volunteers beforehand by having a challenge box. The children who want to be involved in a challenge put their name and team in the box, and you choose them before the start of each day. This can save valuable time. Choose team leader volunteers beforehand, too. **NB:** You will need to warn your volunteers that they may get a little wet!

Day One: Creation appreciation!

Theme illustration

Display some manufactured items, such as a guitar on a stand, a chair, a book or whatever is available. Say to the children:

- If I were to say to you that nobody made this guitar, would you believe me?
- If I were to say to you that nobody made this chair, would you believe me?
- If I were to say to you that nobody made this book, would you believe me?

Of course someone made each one of these items!

Next, introduce a skill, such as balloon modelling, or use an available skill within your leadership group, such as pottery. Show a product of that skill, such as a balloon model or a piece of pottery. Say to the children, 'If I were to say to you that this balloon (pot) has always looked like this, would you believe me?'

Ask for some volunteers and give each one a modelling balloon (or a piece of clay). Make a balloon model (or a pot—especially effective if you have a potter's wheel). Now invite the children to make a balloon (or a pot). You may need to help the children, especially to blow up a balloon.

Say, 'See how something that looked like a flat worm (shapeless lump) has been transformed into this model by the creative hands of our volunteers.' Point out that all the material things we see around us have been made by someone.

The world is amazing! It has been perfectly designed and put together by God—the Master Creator. So let's appreciate the wonderful world he has made for us. Let's give God our creation appreciation.

Team challenge

Ask for two volunteer members from each team. Explain that, later, everyone will be hearing the story about God making our wonderful world, especially the animals. Mention some of the more extraordinary members of the animal world, such as the star-nosed mole, the jellyfish and the giraffe.

Give the pair from each team some newspaper and a reel of sticky tape. Ask them to imagine what a giraffe would look like if they had made it. Then ask each pair to make a giraffe out of the newspaper. The tallest and most life-like giraffe, which is able to stand up without falling over, will be the winner. Give the teams four minutes to complete their creation. Ready, steady, go! Encourage the children to cheer their team on.

Day Two: Creation's crown!

Theme illustration

Start by saying that the human body is amazing, especially the human brain. For example, the ear can hear the tiniest of sounds, and the brain can instantly recognize that sound. Play some sounds for the children to listen to—for example, animal noises, the sound of a train, a helicopter, a ticking clock and so on from a sound effects CD, or different sounds on a keyboard with sampler facilities. Our ears are amazing and do a very important job.

Next, take a soft football or a football marked as a globe. Bounce the ball and catch it. Explain that when we bounce a ball, different parts of our body are working together. Our eyes see the ball and our ears hear it bounce. Our brain sends a message to our body and our legs to keep us balanced and in control of the ball, and to our hands so that we can reach out and make contact with the ball. There is so much going on at the same time. It would be very difficult to program a robot to perform these 'simple' actions.

In the same way, we can use our eyes to focus on the world. We see the world, we are part of the world, but often we just don't notice how fantastic the world around us is. Bounce the ball around the room, so that different children can join in by bouncing it to a neighbour. (This is particularly effective if you have a globe-style football.) Encourage the children to think of all the different parts of the body that are working together as they pass the ball from person to person.

The body and brain are amazing! We are amazing! There is nothing in the universe that absorbs so much information or learns so much as a human being. We have been carefully designed and created by God and we are the crown of his creation. We have been made in his image, but each one of us is unique. Isn't God amazing?

Team challenge

Set up a short activity course and award points for completion of each activity. For example, first of all, the volunteers have to bounce a ball a short way (using their hands and their coordination skills). Award a point for each accurate bounce of the ball. Second, they have to do some simple mental arithmetic (using their brain power). Award a point for each sum they calculate correctly.

Finally, they have to throw some soft balls into a bucket (using their eyes and accuracy skills). Award a point for each ball that lands in the bucket.

Invite one member from each team to take the challenge in turn. The volunteer who completes the course with the highest scores wins.

Ask the children, 'If (name of winning volunteer) had been a monkey, would they have still won?' Point out that they would have struggled to bounce the ball, had no chance with the mental arithmetic and probably would have missed the bucket completely. Point out that monkeys are very clever in many ways but they can never achieve what human beings can achieve. The Bible tells us that human beings have been made in the image of God. We can think things through and work things out. We are creative and innovative. Each one of us is amazing and we need to treat others with respect, remembering that each person has been made in God's image.

Day Three: Careless whispers!

Theme illustration

Ask for approximately ten volunteers to play a game of Chinese Whispers. Alternatively, if you have a smaller number of children, you could include everyone and send the whisper right round the room.

Stand the children in a line side by side. Whisper a sentence into the ear of the first person in the line. For example, 'God's creation is a sensation; I'm sure you agree that there is nothing quite so amazing as you and me!' The first volunteer then whispers the sentence into the ear of the person next to them and so on down the line until the message reaches the last person. Ask the last person in the line to repeat what was whispered into their ear.

If the message is different from the original sentence, point out that it is easy to make a mistake and get things wrong. Yesterday we thought about how amazing human beings are, but today we're going to hear about the biggest mistake in history and how we've continued to get things wrong ever since.

Team challenge

Ask for three volunteers from each team. Blindfold each of them. Set up a simple obstacle course, such as a bench to climb over, a table to crawl under, a hoop to climb through and a cone to touch to finish. Stand each team in a line, with each person holding on to the shoulders of the person in front. Tell the person at the front that you want them to lead their team through the course. As the person at the front is also blindfolded, this will prove to be an impossible task. Encourage the children to cheer for their teams. Make sure no one can see or remove their blindfold. Have adult leaders to hand to prevent anyone from getting hurt.

Next, remove the blindfold of the first person in each team, but leave the other team members blindfolded. Now, on the word 'Go!' the person at the front has to lead his or her team through the course. The first team to finish is the winning team.

Thank the volunteers and ask them to rejoin their teams. Explain that today we are going to hear a story about how the very people made in God's image turned their backs on God and disobeyed him. Ever since, it has been as though we are blindfolded. We do not know where we are going and we stumble in the darkness. Throughout history, people have tried to lead others, but it is like the blind leading the blind. Only with God can we see the way; he is our guiding light.

Day Four: Enough's enough!

Theme illustration

Ask for a volunteer. This person needs to be someone who doesn't mind getting wet. They will also need to be determined. Sit the volunteer in a chair and give him or her a fully loaded water pistol. Tell your volunteer that you are going to test his or her patience. Will they be able to resist using the water pistol? Explain that you are going to instruct four different people to take it in turns to try to annoy the volunteer. When this happens, the volunteer has two choices: he or she can either shoot the annoying person with water or ignore what that person is doing. The volunteer is not allowed to move from the spot. How long will they last?

1 Give a small bowl of water to the first person and invite them to flick water into the face of the volunteer. Will the volunteer resist or will they shoot with the water pistol?
2 Give a small canister of crazy foam to the second person and invite them to paint a beard on the volunteer with the foam. Will the volunteer resist or will they shoot the water pistol?
3 Invite the third person to ruffle the volunteer's hair. Will the volunteer resist or will they use the water pistol?
4 Invite the fourth person to tickle the volunteer. If the volunteer continues to resist, encourage the fourth person to continue tickling until the volunteer can stand it no longer and either moves away or uses the water pistol.

Point out that if someone deliberately tries to annoy you, it is probably best to ignore them, in which case they will probably leave you alone. If that person continues to bother you, there comes a time when you must take action. Enough is enough! The best thing to do is to tell someone you trust that this person is deliberately trying to annoy you, so that the problem can be sorted out.

When God made our wonderful world, he wanted us to look after his creation, so he put us in charge. But look at the mess we have made! We are cruel to animals, we destroy their natural habitats, we destroy the wonderful forests that give life to our world, and we destroy each other by the things we say, think and do. The story of Adam and Eve was just the beginning. After that, people got worse and worse until before long, they had become wholly wicked and selfish. Finally, God said, 'Enough is enough!' and he took action to save his world.

Team challenge

Ask for two volunteers from each team who don't mind getting wet. Ask one volunteer from each pair to lie on his or her back. Place a towel and a tray on the chest of each of the volunteers who are lying down and then place a plastic cup on the tray. Give the other team member a jug of water and invite them to tip some water into the cup. They then place a piece of card on top of the cup and put another plastic cup on top of the card. This cup is also filled with water and another card placed on top. The team that makes the highest tower of cups before the cups fall is the winning team. Encourage the children to cheer their team mates on.

When the challenge is over, help the volunteers to dry off and ask them to rejoin their teams. Point out that enough is enough. You can't keep piling plastic cups full of water on top of each other without making the tower fall down. Adam and Eve disobeyed God, so did their children and so did their children's children. Each generation turned its back on God, and things went from bad to worse: people were selfish and cruel to each other. Finally, God said, 'Enough is enough!' and he took action to save his world. Later on, we are going hear the story about what God did to save his world.

Day Five: The Master's plan

Theme illustration

Ask for a 'fit', athletic volunteer. Tell them that this is an opportunity to show everyone how fit and sporting they really are. Ask them to start by giving us ten star jumps, holding a cup of water. They must try not to spill the water. Excellent! Now ask them to jump around in a circle four times on one leg, still holding the cup of water. Great! Now ask them to do five sit-ups, still holding the cup of water. Wonderful! Next, ask them to do four press-ups, still holding the cup of water.

Enough's enough! It was difficult enough at the start, but to do press-ups while holding a cup of water is virtually impossible.

Not being a robot is great, but there is just one big snag: however hard we try, we keep getting things wrong. It seems impossible not to mess up; we just can't help ourselves. God has given us the Master Designer's instruction book to help to show us the right way. God's book tells us all about God's master plan for his people and for us today.

Team challenge

Beforehand, photocopy three pictures for each team, each showing a different type of robot. Stick the pictures on to coloured card, using a different colour for each set of pictures (if your teams have been allocated colours, use these colours). Hide the pictures around the room and make up a set of instructions or a map for each team, showing where their three pictures are hidden. Ask for a volunteer from each team.

Explain to the volunteers that you have hidden three pictures of robots in their team's colours around the room. The volunteers' job is to find their three coloured robots without any help from the rest of the children or team. Give each team volunteer a master plan with the instructions and a map of where their robots are hidden, but tell them it is up to them whether or not they use the plan. Ask for complete silence while the volunteers try to find their pictures. If desired, you could play 'Mission Impossible' style music at this point. The person who finds their three robots first is the winner.

Point out that the job of finding the robots would have been much harder for each of the volunteers without the master plan, and therefore it would have been silly for them not to use it. Explain that God has given us the Bible to tell us all about his master plan for the world. He has done this because he loves us and he wants us to live happy and fulfilled lives. His instructions for our lives help us to be the best people we can be, and it would be crazy to ignore them. If we follow the Master's plan, we will arrive at God's final destination and receive the reward of eternal life.

The Watt family daily dramas

The Watt family adventure serial drama has proved to be a real winner in holiday club programmes. Children love the different characters and can't wait for the next adventure the following day, proving the formula to be a real incentive for the children to return. Although the drama does have links with the main theme, the primary aim is that it should be fun, rather than being taken too seriously.

Drama tips

Many of the following drama tips are also useful for those telling the Bible narrations.

- Start practising a good month or two before the holiday club. I recommend a minimum of six one-hour practices. The first practice will involve choosing who will play which character and reading through the whole script to get into the storyline. You may choose to record this read-through and make copies for each member of the cast. This is a good technique for learning lines quickly.

- Project your voice: speak out loud and clear. Don't turn your back to the audience when speaking. It is better to face the audience and turn your head to the side when speaking to another character.

- A technician can be useful. Background music or sound effects can add to the atmosphere, but don't make them so loud that the actors can't be heard.

- If you are playing the part of a baddie, try to be a nice, cheeky baddie rather than a very loud, aggressive one. Little children scare easily.

- Don't rush lines. Often, jokes are lost because the delivery isn't clear. The Watt family scripts have been designed to be short and easy to learn, but you need to make the Watt family come to life through plenty of movement. It is useful if someone with experience in drama can come to your rehearsals to watch and direct you in the delivery of lines and stage blocking. Constructive criticism can help to bring the drama to life.

- Think about movement, facial expression, entrances and exits. If there is a chase scene, work out a routine and decide whether you need to have some 'chase' music playing in the background. Often, children find this type of humour funnier than the actual lines.

- Think about your set and costumes. Don't leave costumes and props to the last minute. Don't forget your local toyshop and costume shop in your search for costumes and props, but try the Internet, too. For example, www.hawkin.com can provide bubble blower guns (ideal for Rick), www.partybox.co.uk supplies wigs and costumes and www.sound-effects-library.com have a full range of sound effect CDs.

- Those playing the parts of robots need to move in a slightly rigid way. When turning, robot characters need to start with both feet together. When turning right, the robot's head needs to turn to the right first (like a soldier making a 'right turn'). Then, with the weight of the right foot on the heel, and the weight of the left foot on the toe, the character can easily turn to the right. Once the turn has been made, the robot takes the first step with the left foot and can start to walk slowly but steadily, with his or her arms coming right up to right angles.

- Use either black sunglasses (shades) or mime masks, which are now readily available in many craft shops, for the robot's headgear. The masks can be painted silver. Robots could be dressed in black, silver or a combination of black and silver. Dryer vent duct from a local DIY store makes great robot arms and legs. Finish the hands with an old pair of gloves and the feet with shoebox shoes, covered with tin foil. Spraypaint the vent duct and gloves silver or a combination of black and silver. Finish the costume with a black or grey T-shirt. Try to make all your robots as similar as possible, but don't make them look too scary.

Overview

The Watt family are a wacky, fun-loving family. Their *Razzamatazz Robots* adventure drama is performed in a fast-moving, fun style. Day One introduces the main characters and sets the scene; on Day Two we meet Professor Roly Rolo and his amazing Razzamatazz robots. Professor Rolo makes the Watt family an offer they can't refuse and everything seems to be going very well for Grandma, Rick and Wendy… or is it? On Day Three, Professor Rolo reveals his really mean, dishonest and dastardly plan. On Day Four, Grandma and Rick get themselves into a fix—will Wendy be able to rescue them? Finally, on Day Five, the master plan wins the day.

The storyline adheres lightly to the daily themes, but the intention is not to draw too strong a parallel; just have fun and make sure your audience does, too.

NB: The scene setting is an empty stage unless otherwise stated.

Day One: Creation appreciation!

Cast
✜ Narrator
✜ Grandma Watt
✜ Rick Watt
✜ Wendy Watt
✜ Ro Botwatt

Props
Bubble gun and packet of Rolos (for Rick), table, remote control unit, boiled egg, egg cup, screwdriver, advertising leaflet, bag of flour, mixing bowl, the Watt family theme tune and a CD player (optional)

The scene is the Watt family's kitchen. There is a table in the middle of the stage. On the table, there is a boiled egg in an egg cup, a remote control unit, a screwdriver, a bag of flour, a bowl and an advertising leaflet for Professor Rolo's Razzamatazz Robots. Enter Narrator.

Narrator: Grandma, Rick and Wendy Watt have decided to design and build their own robot. They are very excited because they have finally finished the robot and have programmed it to bake a cake. This is the big test!

Enter Grandma and Wendy Watt.

Wendy: Hello, everyone! *(She delivers the next lines very quickly in one breath)* I'm Wendy, Wendy Watt. Everyone says I talk a lot, but I'm sure you don't think I talk a lot, because I don't really talk a lot! I only talk if nobody else is talking, because I might as well talk when no one else is talking, as no one else is talking then. Oh, and we're building our very own robot. It's very, very, very exciting!

Grandma: Put a sock in it, Wendy!

Wendy: What, in the robot?

Grandma: No, dear, I mean stop talking! I can't get a word in edgeways with all your chatter. Hello, everyone. I'm Grandma Watt and we're building our very own robot. He's called Ro Botwatt!

Enter Rick, shooting his bubble gun at the children.

Rick: It's Watt, Rick Watt. I'm cool and cra-a-zy!

Wendy: He thinks he's James Bond!

Enter Robot.

Grandma: Ha, here comes Ro Botwatt! Watch this, this should be good. I've programmed him to carefully pick up an egg.

Grandma Watt picks up the remote control and points it at the robot. The robot walks over to the table, but struggles to locate the egg. He jerks his hand to different positions on the table and looks confused.

Grandma: Oh dear, Ro Botwatt can't find the egg. I need to make some fine adjustments. I'd better freeze the program.

Grandma presses a button on the remote control. The robot freezes. Grandma picks up the screwdriver and pretends to open a flap on the back of the robot and make some adjustments. The robot makes funny faces as though it is rather uncomfortable.

Grandma: That's done the trick, it should work fine now.

Grandma presses the remote control again and the robot begins to move. This time, he finds the egg.

Grandma: Now, let's see how carefully he can pick up the egg.

The robot picks up the egg and crushes it in his hands, making a terrible mess.

Wendy: Oh, yuck!
Rick: *(Excitedly)* Cor! Smashing!
Grandma: Oh dear, oh dear!
Wendy: Your egg test has failed, Grandma! But watch this, I have programmed him to pick up a bag of flour and tip the exact amount into the bowl. This will be good!

Wendy takes the remote control from Grandma and presses a button. The robot slowly picks up the bag of flour and turns towards the bowl. Wendy looks excited.

Wendy: Look! He's picked up the bag of flour and has turned to the bowl. This is going to be great!

The robot tips the flour out on to the table, completely missing the bowl. Grandma tries to hide her grin of delight.

Rick: Ha! Wendy, you failed too!
Wendy: All right, all right! I do think the 'flour in the bowl' test is a particularly difficult one, though!
Rick: Well, you two have spoiled my test, because I programmed him to put his hands in the bowl and mix the flour and eggs together. *(Getting excited as the robot picks up the bowl)* Wow! He's picked up the bowl! It's going to work; it's going to work!

The robot puts the empty bowl on his head and spins round and round on the spot, going faster and faster until he falls to the ground.

Grandma: Oh no, he's malfunctioned!
Wendy: Ha! You failed too, Rick. Ro Botwatt didn't mix the cake, he mixed himself. What a mess!
Rick: I told you this would happen, didn't I, Grandma? Why can't we just buy one of Professor Roly Rolo's Razzamatazz Robots?

Wendy: Oooh, yes! He's built hundreds of them!
Grandma: Yes, I know. He has them rolling off the production line right now. They all look exactly the same. I thought it would be good to make our own unique robot, with its own character, but it's proving to be more difficult than I thought.
Rick: Can we buy one of Professor Rolo's Razzamatazz Robots, then? Can we, can we?
Wendy: Ple-e-ase?
Grandma: Oh, I don't know. There's something about that Rolo chappy and his Razzamatazz Robots that I just don't trust.
Rick: What? Not trust Prof Rolo's professional robots?
Grandma: I'm not sure about his TV advert and his slogan.
Wendy: Oh, but it's really cool!
Rick: Yes, let's sing it to everyone.

Wendy and Rick sing to the tune of 'Heads, shoulders, knees and toes'.

Wendy/Rick: Human friends just let you down, let you down.
Human friends just make you frown, make you frown.
But Razzamatazz Robots are so very fine.
They'll obey you all the time, all the time!

Let's sing it again!

They repeat the song, encouraging the children to join in and going faster and faster with each repetition.

Grandma: *(Putting her hands over her ears)* That's enough! I don't like that song at the best of times! *(Picking up the leaflet about Razzamatazz Robots)* I don't like what it says about them in this leaflet, either. *(Reading from the leaflet)* 'Do your friends argue with you? Razzamatazz Robots won't! Do your friends disobey you? Razzamatazz Robots won't! They'll make your bed, tidy your room and always have time for you! You'll never need another human friend again!'
Rick: What's wrong with that?
Wendy: It sounds wonderful! There will be no more arguments, Grandma.
Rick: Yeah, Grandma, have a Rolo. *(Offers Grandma a Rolo, but she ignores him)*
Grandma: *(Shaking her head and muttering)* Oh, I don't know. I just don't know.
Wendy: *(Taking a Rolo from Rick)* Mmmm, lovely, thanks, Rick.

31

Grandma:	(Continuing to shake her head and mutter) Oh dear, oh dear…

Rick shrugs his shoulders and puts the Rolos back in his pocket.

Narrator:	Can Grandma be persuaded to buy one of Roly Rolo's Razzamatazz Robots? Can Rolo's robots really be trusted? Find out in the next exciting episode of… the Watt family's Razzamatazz Robots adventure.

Play the Watt family theme tune.

Day Two: Creation's crown!

Cast
- Narrator
- Grandma Watt
- Rick Watt
- Wendy Watt
- Shop assistant
- URACM robot
- URAGP robot
- URAWC robot
- URAHD robot
- Professor Roly Rolo
- URACD robot (NB: this person should learn some cool dance moves to perform on stage)

All robots are dressed exactly the same: see page 29 for costume suggestions.

Props
Bubble gun and packet of Rolos (for Rick), table, remote control unit, wooden spoon, mixing bowl, bucket of water and sponge, comb and a pair of scissors, the Watt family theme tune and a CD player (optional)

The scene is the Razzamatazz Robots shop. The table from Day One can become the shop counter.

Narrator:	Grandma, Rick and Wendy decided to build their own robot but it crashed out; it malfunctioned. So they've decided to go down to the Razzamatazz Robots shop to see what's on offer.

Assistant:	(In a typically 'over the top' sales style) Welcome, welcome! You are so, so welcome, little old lady and family!
Grandma:	We are thinking of buying a robot.
Assistant:	Well, you've come to the right place, yes, the r-i-g-h-t place! We have a wide range of g-r-e-a-t robots available here today! Let me introduce you to the first robot. (Picking up a remote control and looking off stage) Engage URACM.

Robot walks in wearing a badge saying, 'URACM Razzamatazz Robot'. The robot is carrying a wooden spoon and a bowl.

Assistant:	This is our latest range, the UR series. This is the URACM robot.
Rick:	Cool!
Wendy:	What does URACM stand for?
Assistant:	(Over-kindly) Well, little girl, UR obviously stands for 'you are' and ACM stands for 'a cake maker': the 'You are a cake maker' robot! Yes, this Razzamatazz Robot makes g-r-e-a-t cakes! Show them your stirring move, URACM! (Robot mimes stirring a cake in the bowl) See, what a g-r-e-a-t action!
Grandma:	Sounds good to me. We'll take it.
Assistant:	Hey, not so fast, little old lady!
Grandma:	Watch it! Not so much of the 'little old lady'!
Assistant:	We have far more g-r-e-a-t Razzamatazz Robots to show you!
Grandma:	More?
Assistant:	Oh yes! (Pointing off stage with the remote control) Engage URAGP.

Another robot enters. It walks very quickly on to the stage and heads straight for Grandma. The URACM robot carries on pretending to make a cake.

Grandma:	Here! He's coming straight towards me!
Assistant:	Yes, I think he wants to play 'chase' (or 'tick', 'it' or 'tag', depending on what you call the game) with you.

The robot picks up speed and chases Grandma Watt round the stage.

Grandma:	Get off!
Rick:	Cool!
Assistant:	(Pointing the remote control at the robot) I'll freeze the program.

Robot freezes.

Grandma:	(Out of breath) He looks exactly the same as the last one!

Reproduced with permission from *Razzamatazz Robots Holiday Club!* published by BRF 2008 (978 1 84101 577 4)

Assistant:	*(Excitedly)* Of course! This is the next model in our UR range: the URAGP!
Wendy:	And what does URAGP stand for?
Assistant:	*(Over-kindly)* Well, little girl, this robot has been programmed to play games. If you are looking for someone to partner you whenever you feel like playing a game, the URAGP is the robot for you! URAGP is our 'You are a games player' robot!
Grandma:	Does it bake cakes as well?
Assistant:	Well, er, no. This is the URAGP, not the URACM. *(Pause. Points the remote control off stage)* But let me show you the URAWC!

A third robot enters, carrying a bucket of water and sponge. It makes straight for Grandma Watt and starts washing her face and glasses with the sponge.

Grandma:	Get off, you horrible robot!
Rick:	These robots are so cool!
Wendy:	*(To Assistant)* And URAWC stands for…?
Grandma:	Sounds like a toilet robot! Yuck!
Assistant:	*(In a condescending tone)* URAWC is our 'You are a window cleaner' robot.
Grandma:	Let me guess… cleans windows, but doesn't bake a cake or play games.
Assistant:	That is correct, little old lady. *(Pointing remote control off stage)* We also have the URAHD.

A fourth robot enters, carrying a comb and scissors, and immediately starts to ruffle Grandma Watt's hair.

Grandma:	*(To robot)* Get off! They're all picking on me!
Rick:	These robots are really, really cool!
Wendy:	*(To sales assistant)* URAHD?
Assistant:	The URAHD is our 'You are a hairdresser' robot. *(Sales pitch style)* So which is it to be: the URACM, the URAGP, the URAWC or the URAHD? Or, of course, we have a g-r-e-a-t deal for you today: buy three; get one free!

All robots are moving around, acting out their tasks. They are taking up lots of space and weaving in and out between the Watt family members.

Rick:	Cool, we'll take them all! Would you like a Rolo? *(Offers one to assistant, who ignores him)*
Wendy:	*(Taking a Rolo from Rick)* Mmmm, lovely, thanks, Rick.

Grandma:	Hang on, hang on! You mean that each robot can only do one task?
Assistant:	Of course!
Grandma:	But we need *one* robot to do *all* the household chores!
Assistant:	Technology isn't that advanced yet. You've been watching too many science fiction movies, little old lady! But don't forget our g-r-e-a-t special offer to buy three and get one free.
Grandma:	We've only got a small house. We wouldn't be able to move with all these robots in action!
Assistant:	*(Sales pitch style)* Exactly, exactly, exactly! Dear lady, you are *so*, so right. You wouldn't need to get out of your own bed. The robots will do *all* the chores for you. Just think how blissful that would be!
Rick:	This is so cool! Can we take advantage of the special offer, Grandma?
Grandma:	No, we can't! I wouldn't be able to move in my own house!

Enter Professor Rolo.

Assistant:	Wow! Would you believe it? The legendary Professor Roly Rolo—the inventor of the UR robot series—has just walked into our shop! This is g-r-e-a-t!

The Watt family turn to look.

Prof Rolo:	Well, well, well, what have we here? I have arrived just at the right time. I couldn't help overhearing you, little old lady. *(Grandma goes to interrupt, but thinks better of it)* I have just the thing for you! I have just invented a single robot that can do all the chores you can think of. I have named it the URACD. This is the super-duper ultimate robot of your dreams. *(Over-kindly)* Just right for this little old lady and her family!

Enter the robot, performing some cool dance moves as it comes on stage.

Prof Rolo:	As you can see, this robot moves far more smoothly than my prototypes. It has far more flexibility.
Wendy:	Wow, now this is truly amazing!
Prof Rolo:	And, as you are such valued customers, I will allow you to take this robot home with you free of charge! What do you say to that?
Grandma:	We'll have to think about it!
Rick:	What my Grandma meant to say was—we'll have it! Coooooool!

Wendy:	Yes, thank you! This is truly splendid!

Grandma looks doubtful, but the Watt family exit with the URACD robot.

Prof Rolo:	(*To audience in sneaky voice*) Ha, ha, ha! Little do they know that with my new line of robots I plan to rule the world.
Narrator:	Excuse me, did you say 'rule the world'?
Prof Rolo:	(*Looking caught out*) Err… no, I said, 'It can iron a shirt!'
Narrator:	Oh no, you didn't!
Prof Rolo:	Oh yes, I did!
Narrator:	(*Encouraging audience to join in*) Oh no, you didn't!
Prof Rolo:	I can assure you I did. You can trust me.
Narrator:	Right, so it can iron a shirt? Now that will be useful!

Professor Rolo and the shop assistant exit in the manner of villains, encouraging the audience to react as they go.

Narrator:	Oh dear, I don't like the look of this! What dastardly plan does Professor Rolo have in store? Will the URACD robot be able to iron a shirt? Will we ever know what URACD stands for? Find out in the next exciting episode of… the Watt family's Razzamatazz Robots adventure.

Play the Watt family theme tune.

Day Three: Careless whispers!

Cast
Narrator
Professor Roly Rolo
Rick Watt
Grandma Watt
Several Razzamatazz robots

Props
Bubble gun and packet of Rolos (for Rick), remote control unit, the Watt family theme tune and a CD player (optional)

Narrator:	One whole year has gone by since the Watt family took home their URACD Razzamatazz Robot and, surprisingly, nothing terrible has happened. I was sure

that Professor Roly Rolo—the inventor of the amazing UR Razzamatazz Robots— was up to something, but I was wrong. The Watt family love their robot.

Enter Professor Rolo.

Prof Rolo:	(*In a charming voice*) Oh (*name of narrator*), did you really think I had a dastardly plan up my sleeve?
Narrator:	(*Ashamed*) Yes, I must admit I did. I thought you were up to something really mean, dishonest and dastardly, but I was wrong.
Prof Rolo:	(*Surprised*) Me? Up to something really mean, dishonest and dastardly?
Narrator:	Yes, how silly of me to think such a thing!
Prof Rolo:	No, not at all, not at all! In fact, you're absolutely right! I do have a really mean, dishonest and dastardly plan up my sleeve. (*Gives a sneaky laugh*)
Narrator:	(*Laughing nervously*) Oh, Professor, you're such a tease!
Prof Rolo:	(*Menacingly*) Don't interrupt! No one can stop my really mean, dishonest and dastardly plan from working! (*Excitedly and in an extremely nasty voice*) You see, I am now the richest and most powerful man in the world, and I intend to rule the world! Almost every home in the country now owns one of my amazing Razzamatazz Robots. I am a household name. People have become lazy because my robots do absolutely everything for them. Most people just stay in bed; they never go out and they rely totally on my robots to do all the housework. People can't even bake a cake any more; they rely completely on my amazing robots. (*Sneaky laugh*) Ha, ha, ha!

Enter Rick and Grandma Watt. They burst in suddenly through the door.

Rick:	(*Very excited to see Professor Rolo*) Hey, Professor Rolo! You are the coolest dude ever! Have a Rolo (*Offers one to the Professor, who ignores him*)
Grandma:	(*Takes a Rolo from Rick*) Mmmm, lovely, thanks, Rick. Oh yes, we love Albert so much! It's his first birthday today, so he's having a lie in!
Prof Rolo:	Albert? Who's Albert?
Rick:	Don't you recognize us? We're the Watt family.
Prof Rolo:	Who?

Reproduced with permission from *Razzamatazz Robots Holiday Club!* published by BRF 2008 (978 1 84101 577 4) **34**

Grandma:	No, not Who, dear, Watt. We are the Watt family, the Whos live down the road. Exactly a year ago today, you gave us Albert.
Prof Rolo:	*(Starting to get cross and shout)* Who is Albert?
Rick:	He's our URACD—the Razzamatazz Robot you gave us.
Grandma:	But we call him Albert.
Rick:	We named him after Einstein, because he's so clever.
Prof Rolo:	*(Slowly)* R-i-g-h-t… and where did you say he was?
Grandma:	He's having a lie in. He works so hard, we wanted to give him a special birthday treat.
Prof Rolo:	One of my Razzamatazz Robots in bed?
Rick:	Yes, we've persuaded him to stay in bed while Wendy makes a secret birthday cake for him.
Prof Rolo:	Cake? No one bakes cakes any more! In fact, no one does any work any more, because my robots do it for them.
Grandma:	Oh yes, we thought that at first. We were becoming very lazy. Albert did everything. If I tried to do any work, Albert took over.
Rick:	But Grandma sorted him with one of her special chips.
Prof Rolo:	A special chip?
Grandma:	Yes. It was tough going, but eventually I managed to open him up and give him one of my chips.
Prof Rolo:	Stop, stop, stop! I've heard enough. If this gets out, you'll ruin my really mean, dishonest and dastardly plan! You must be stopped! My Razzamatazz Robots will stop you!

Prof Rolo points off stage with a remote control and suddenly several robots appear.

Prof Rolo:	Robots, the Watt family must be stopped!
Grandma:	I think Professor Rolo has lost the plot!
Prof Rolo:	Get them!

Rick dives to the ground, rolls over to the left three times and back, crawls backwards under the table and quickly pulls out his bubble gun. He shoots at the robots, then crawls, using just his elbows, under the legs of several robots. Next, he stands up and starts to shoot at the robots again. His acrobatics are all accomplished to suitable music, such as the theme to 'Mission Impossible' or something similar. One of the robots carries on chasing Rick, while another robot chases Grandma, who is running round in a figure of eight. Suddenly, the music stops and everyone freezes.

Narrator:	Oh no, has Professor Rolo lost the plot? Is his plan really mean, dishonest and dastardly? Will Rick and Grandma escape from the robots? Will Wendy's cake rise? Find out in the next exciting episode of… the Watt family's Razzamatazz Robots adventure.

Play the Watt family theme tune.

Day Four: Enough's enough!

Cast
Narrator
Wendy Watt
Grandma Watt
Rick Watt
Two Razzamatazz robots
Professor Roly Rolo

Props
Bubble gun and packet of Rolos (for Rick), sponge cake, rope, remote control unit, a torch and a large remote control with an impressive front panel (for Professor Rolo), the Watt family theme tune and a CD player (optional)

Narrator:	Oh no! It seems that Professor Rolo really does have a mean, dishonest and dastardly plan. Rick and Grandma Watt are being chased by Razzamatazz Robots. But, meanwhile, back at the Watt family home…

Enter Wendy, proudly holding a large sponge cake.

Wendy:	*(Showing everyone the cake)* Look, everyone, I've made a special cake for Albert, our robot best friend. He's having a bit of a lie in at the moment. Grandma and Rick have gone to see the wonderful Professor Rolo to see if he can recommend something nice to buy Albert for his birthday. He's such a sweet man, that Professor Rolo, isn't he?

 Reproduced with permission from *Razzamatazz Robots Holiday Club!* published by BRF 2008 (978 1 84101 577 4)

Leaders in the audience encourage the children to respond by shouting, 'Oh no, he isn't!'

Wendy: *(Surprised)* Oh yes, he is!

All: Oh no, he isn't!

Wendy: *(Continuing with the banter for a few minutes)* Oh yes, he is! He's the kindest, sweetest person, because he gave us Albert. He's also very, very clever, because he invented the Razzamatazz Robots in the first place. How can you say he isn't? Is there something I haven't been told?

Wendy encourages the children to put up their hands and tell her what has happened.

Wendy: What? Grandma and Rick are being chased by robots? I'd better get down there now!

Exit Wendy in a hurry.

Narrator: Meanwhile, Professor Rolo and his robots have captured Grandma and Rick. They are now tied up and are being questioned by Professor Rolo. If we listen carefully, we just might be able to hear what is being said.

Enter Grandma and Rick Watt, led on stage by two robots, who tie them up and make them sit down. Professor Rolo shines a torch in Rick's face.

Rick: Oi! Why are you shining that torch in my face?

Prof Rolo: Because I am interrogating you, of course. *(Shining the torch in Grandma's face)* Now then, little old lady, yesterday you said that you have invented a special silicon chip and inserted it into my robot's circuitry program. Tell me, how did you do it? I demand you tell me about the chip!

Grandma: *(Very confused)* What? I said I had invented a special silicon chip and inserted it into your robot's circuitry program? Gosh! I didn't know I was that clever.

Prof Rolo: Yes, you are obviously a genius like me.

Grandma: Ooh, thank you very much! That's probably the nicest thing anybody has ever said to me.

Prof Rolo: Good! Now tell me!

Grandma: I can't.

Prof Rolo: *(Getting crosser and crosser)* Tell me!

Grandma: I can't.

Prof Rolo: Why can't you?

Grandma: Because you didn't say 'please'.

Prof Rolo: What? *(Pause)* Oh, very well… Pleeeessssse!

Grandma: No, I still can't. What with all this talk of silicon chip circuitry and reprogramming, I'm a very confused grandma!

Rick: Grandma, just tell him. Then we can all go home. *(To Professor Rolo)* Grandma makes the best chips in the world.

Prof Rolo: Yes, I must agree. A chip that is capable of changing my robots is a very powerful chip indeed. Do you know the circuitry?

Rick: Do you mean, does she know how she makes them?

Prof Rolo: Yes, yes! Tell me!

Rick: Well, she chops up potatoes into chips and puts them into the deep fat fryer. That's right, isn't it, Grandma?

Prof Rolo: Ho, ho, very funny. You can't treat me like a fool. I'll get the truth out of you somehow, you'll see. Deep fat fried chips, indeed. You may think you're clever, but you're not as clever as me, Grandma Watt.

Grandma: *(Confused)* What have I done now?

Enter Wendy. She creeps in quietly and listens to what is going on. She stays hidden for the first part of the Professor Rolo's following speech, then slowly creeps up and unties Rick and Grandma.

Prof Rolo: Somehow you have discovered my plan. *(Passionately)* As you *(looking at Grandma)* well know, I can control every Razzamatazz Robot in the world.

Grandma and Rick look at each other and shrug their shoulders. They clearly have no idea what Professor Rolo is talking about.

Prof Rolo: By using this… *(revealing a large remote control with impressive front panel).* When I switch this on, it activates my satellite in space, which sends a signal to all my robots. The signal is for the command to attack! On that command, my robots will capture every human being.

Wendy starts to creep towards Rick and Grandma but, every time Professor Rolo turns to look at Grandma or Rick, Wendy has to hide behind a chair or a robot. You will need to work out a routine for this.

Prof Rolo: Then, using my satellite, I will broadcast a message into every home.

He looks at Grandma, then looks away again. Wendy hides, then creeps closer when he looks away.

Prof Rolo: I will demand that everyone gives me all their money!

He looks at Grandma, then looks away again. Once again, Wendy hides, then creeps even closer when he looks away.

Prof Rolo: I can then spend billions and billions on developing the ultimate Razzamatazz Robot. But you…

He turns to Grandma Watt again. Wendy is now hiding behind Grandma and Rick and begins to untie them.

Prof Rolo: … you have not only managed to reprogram your robot so that it is no longer under my control, but also, it will not now respond to my signal.

Robot 1: Intruder alert! Intruder alert!

Both robots start to walk towards Wendy, who suddenly jumps up and runs round and round the robots and Professor Rolo until they all become dizzy and fall to the ground. The robots get jerkily to their feet and continue to chase Wendy round and round the stage. Suddenly Wendy stops and points up.

Wendy: Look!

The first robot looks up. Wendy quickly darts under his legs, causing him to lose his balance. The second robot goes to help and Wendy gives him a gentle push, knocking him straight on top of the first robot. Grandma and Rick give a big cheer as Wendy runs over and finally unties them. All three characters exit.

Prof Rolo: *(Still sprawled on the ground)* Catch them! I haven't finished my speech yet!

Narrator: No time for the rest of your speech today, Professor Rolo! That was a smart move by Wendy, but will the Watt family be able to outrun the robots? Can our heroic team stop Professor Rolo in his tracks? Can they put a stop to his really mean, dishonest and dastardly plan? Find out in the next exciting episode of… the Watt family's Razzamatazz Robots adventure.

Play the Watt family theme tune.

Day Five: The Master's plan

Cast
Narrator
Wendy Watt
Grandma Watt
Rick Watt
Two Razzamatazz robots
Professor Roly Rolo

Props
Bubble gun and packet of Rolos (for Rick), walking stick, toy lightsabre sword, bag of chips, large remote control with an impressive front panel (for Professor Rolo), the Watt family theme tune and a CD player (optional)

Narrator: Welcome back to the Watt family's Razzamatazz Robots adventure! In our last exciting episode, we discovered that Professor Rolo has a really mean, dishonest and dastardly plan up his sleeve. He has found a way to make the ultimate Razzamatazz Robot and rule the world. Rick and Grandma fell into his clutches when Grandma revealed that she was rather good at making chips, but Wendy came to the rescue. Now our three brave heroes are being chased by two of Professor Rolo's Razzamatazz Robots. Have the Watt family done enough to foil the dastardly plan? Will they succeed when the chips are down? Here they come now…

Grandma, Rick and Wendy enter, walking backwards. Rick is shooting his bubble gun at the robots, but the robots haven't given up the chase. Grandma is using her walking stick as a sword and is fighting one of the robots, who is using a toy lightsabre sword. Wendy is wagging her finger at the robots and talking nineteen to the dozen.

Wendy: *(To robot)* How dare you come after us like this? Don't you know who we are? We are the world famous Watt family. I'm Wendy Watt, sister of Rick Watt and granddaughter of Grandma Watt. Everyone says I talk a lot, but I really don't know what they are talking about, because I certainly don't talk a lot! I just talk when no one else is talking!

Robot puts its hands over its ears, but keeps moving forward towards Wendy.

Wendy: Don't you know that we've been on lots and lots and lots of adventures? That's because we are intrepid heroes. You can't beat us, you know!

Rick: *(Stops shooting)* Oh no, my bubble gun has run out of bubbles.

The robot fighting with Grandma Watt grabs her walking stick.

Grandma: It's no good, the Razzamatazz Robots are too strong for us. We can't hold them off any longer. I'm all in! *(Sinking to the floor)* We're beaten this time!

The robots grab the Watt family and hold them. Enter Professor Rolo.

Prof Rolo: Ha, ha, ha! Did you really think you could escape from my amazing Razzamatazz Robots?

Wendy: I'm confused, Professor Rolo. You see, this time yesterday you were my hero because you are the inventor of our wonderful robot, Albert. I thought that anyone who could invent such a wonderful companion and friend must be a wonderful person, but now you're treating us as if we were your enemies.

Prof Rolo: Me, a hero? Did you really think of me as a hero?

Grandma: Oh yes, we did, Professor Rolo. I know many people who are really quite lonely, but you have transformed their lives. You see, although your Razzamatazz Robots aren't humans, for many people they are the next best thing. They help with the household chores and, because they can walk and talk, they make great companions for lonely people everywhere.

Prof Rolo: Exactly! Computers are great, but human beings are incredible, absolutely incredible. I've always been fascinated by the way every part of the human body has an important job to do. There's no doubt that whoever invented human beings is the best inventor, designer and creator ever.

Grandma: We can't argue with that.

Prof Rolo: But that's the problem, people do.

Grandma: Do? Do what?

Prof Rolo: Argue all the time.

Wendy: Not all the time.

Rick: I *never* argue.

Grandma: *(Almost chokes)* Oh yes, you do!

Rick: Oh no, I don't!

All: Oh yes, you do!

Rick: OK, I do! But I wouldn't argue if everyone else would just accept that I'm always right.

Grandma: Oh no, you're not!

Wendy: No! I am!

Rick: Oh no, you're not!

Rick and Wendy both start to argue.

Prof Rolo: You see! I'm right! And that's the reason I've decided to build a robot that's even better than human beings. A super-duper robot that behaves just like a human being, but with the subtle difference that it always does as it is told and never argues. But it's proving to be much harder than I thought.

Grandma: That's because robots are just machines. They are not really alive, so they can never truly take the place of human beings.

Rick: Yes, the world would be a boring place if everyone and everything behaved in exactly the same way as your robots do.

Prof Rolo: *(Angrily)* Are you calling my robots boring?

Rick: Well, they are interesting as far as robots go, but they could never replace real mates and a family that loves and cares for you.

Prof Rolo: I wouldn't know. I have never had time for people. I don't have any friends or a family that loves and cares for me. I've always found that people are just irritating. That's why I've decided to get rid of human beings for good and replace them with my ultimate robots—a world full of robots that always do as I say, never answer back and never argue with me. I will be in control. I will rule the world.

Grandma: *(Rubbing her tummy)* Rumble, rumble!

Prof Rolo: What was that?

Grandma: Ooh, beg pardon—that was my tummy.

Rick: Have a Rolo, Grandma.

Grandma: *(Takes a Rolo from Rick)* Mmmm, lovely, thanks, Rick.

Wendy: *(Taking out a bag of chips)* That reminds me, Grandma. I've brought some of your chips.

Prof Rolo: What? Grandma's special silicon chips? Get them!

The robots try to grab the bag of chips.

Wendy:	Get off! These are for Grandma.

The robots start another chase, which ends when they finally corner Wendy.

Wendy:	Cor, if you're that desperate for one of Grandma's chips, you can have one!

Wendy opens the mouth of one of the robots and feeds it a chip. The robot makes 'yum, yum' noises and shows that it is enjoying the chip.

Prof Rolo:	What? Grandma's special chip really is a potato chip? You've been feeding your robot with potato chips?
Grandma:	And cake!
Prof Rolo:	No wonder Albert doesn't perform the way he's meant to. Robots can't eat food. His insides will be all clogged up. *(Pause)* However, please may I try one? I've never had a potato chip, I have only ever dealt with silicon chips.
Wendy:	You need to get out more!

Prof Rolo:	*(Taking a chip)* Yummy, these really are splendid! Well, I suppose it's time to put my plan into action. Shame, really, I don't think I've ever had such a long chat with anyone before. I talk to my robots, but they don't really chat. I talk to the people who work for me, but they just nod and say, 'Yes, Professor.' I think they are a bit scared of me. But you guys have actually spoken to me as if I was a real human being. You keep asking me questions and you seem really interested in what I have to say.

Rick:	Won't you get bored ruling the world on your own?
Prof Rolo:	You see what I mean? You're always asking questions. For the first time in my life, you have made me doubt my plan. Perhaps human beings aren't so bad after all. I know… *(Looking at Rick)* Rick, *you* can decide. You can be me! *(Handing the super-duper control panel to Rick)* You now have the choice: you can either be the richest, most powerful person in the world, or you can save your family and friends.
Grandma:	Doomed, doomed, we're all doomed!
Rick:	Wow! Me the richest and most powerful person in the world! No one to boss me around! In fact, I will be the one to boss everyone else around. Which button did you say?

Grandma and Wendy look terribly worried.

Wendy:	What are you going to do?
Rick:	I thought that was obvious! *(Everyone freezes and looks worried)* I'm going to let this lot make the decision! *(Pointing to the audience)* Let's have a vote. *(To audience)* If you were me, would you choose to be the richest and most powerful person in the world? Would you choose to get rid of human beings and replace them with a bunch of robots? Or would you choose to keep your friends and family, even though they are far from perfect?

Rick encourages the audience to vote.

Prof Rolo:	But human friends just let you down.
Grandma:	Sometimes, but more often than not, they pick you up when you fall down.
Prof Rolo:	Human beings are greedy and selfish.
Wendy:	Sometimes, but more often than not, they are generous and kind.
Prof Rolo:	Human beings can't be trusted.

Rick walks across to Professor Rolo and hands him the super-duper control panel. Everyone gasps.

Rick:	Professor Rolo, I do believe this is yours. I trust you to make the right decision.

Wendy and Grandma are still looking very worried.

 Reproduced with permission from *Razzamatazz Robots Holiday Club!* published by BRF 2008 (978 1 84101 577 4)

Prof Rolo: *(Looking very pleased with himself)* Oh, Rick, you are such a silly boy. You are so thick, Rick. You could have been quick, Rick, but now I am going to flick, Rick, the super-duper remote control switch, Rick… *(Goes to press the button, but then delivers the next line very slowly)* Hang on a moment… what did you say? You trust me? Trust me? Hang on a tick, Rick! You're a cheeky monkey! You are probably not the cleverest of human beings on the planet, but you have taught me the most important lesson in my life. And you have saved the world at the same time.

Rick: Welcome to the world of living, breathing, real humans, Professor! Have a Rolo… *(Offers the professor a Rolo)*

Prof Rolo: *(Takes a Rolo from Rick)* Mmmm, lovely, thanks, Rick.

Rick offers everyone else in the cast a Rolo, including the robots. Everyone starts being very chummy, slapping each other on the back, sharing Rolos and indulging in general chitchat.

Narrator: Phew! That was a sticky moment. But our heroes have won the day. Robots may be smart, but they can't show love in the way that human beings can. Three cheers for Rick and the caring, sharing Watt family! Hip, hip, hurray!

Play the Watt family theme tune.

NB: See page 83 for another episode of the Watt Family drama, which could be used at a holiday club extra activity or the holiday club Sunday service.

Razzamatazz crafts

Razzamatazz visors or heart shades

You will need:
Visor or heart shades templates on pages 73–74 (one per child) copied on to card, transparent plastic, scissors, coloured pencils, glue or sticky tape.

Cut out the visor or shades and colour them in. Stick the two halves together where shown.

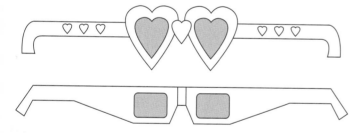

Razzamatazz Robots board game

You will need:
Photocopies of the board game template on page 75 (one per team), copied on to strong card, coloured pencils, scissors, pencils (one per team), coins (one per team).

Give each team a copy of the Razzamatazz Robots board game and a coin. The children play the game by following the instructions on the board. The first team to have all its players reach the winning square is the winning team.

Alternatively, photocopy one board game per child so that the children can take their robot board game home with them.

Box robot

You will need:
Photocopies of the box robot template on page 76 (one per child), copied on to mediumweight card, scissors, coloured pencils, glue, split-pin fasteners, pipe cleaners.

First of all, colour the robot. Next, carefully cut out each piece and assemble the robot by folding and gluing all tabs. Fix base of head to top of body. Affix the wheels to the robot with split-pin fasteners. Use a pipe cleaner to make the arms, making sure that the pipe cleaner is pushed right through the body of the robot.

NB: This model is suitable for children aged seven and above.

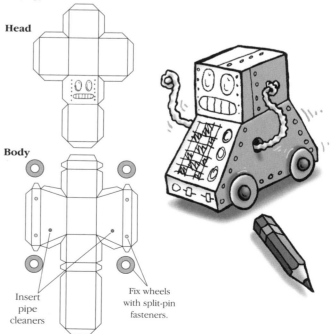

Head

Body

Insert pipe cleaners

Fix wheels with split-pin fasteners.

Razzamatazz Robot outfit

You will need:
Razzamatazz Robot visors (see template on page 73), Razzamatazz Robot headbands (use rainbow headband template on page 79), sturdy card, tin foil, string or ribbon, ruler, scissors, sticky tape or glue (for visor), Climaflex (preformed pipe insulating tube) or reflective radiator foil (for arms and legs), stick-on Velcro fasteners.

To create a Razzamatazz Robot outfit like the one below, make the visor as per the instructions on page 41. Use the headband template from page 79, but cover the whole shape with tin foil. For the torso, cut a rectangle measuring 25cm x 35cm out of mediumweight card. Cut the sides into a 'V' shape, as shown below. Cut out a 'V' shaped neckline. Cover the card with tin foil. Attach string or ribbon as shown to fix the body cover around the child's torso.

Create metallic arm and leg bands out of Climaflex preformed pipe insulating tube or reflective radiator foil (both can be found in most DIY stores). Make separate upper arm, lower arm, upper leg and lower leg sections, so that the child can move his or her joints. Fasten each band with stick-on Velcro.

Razzamatazz mask

You will need:
Photocopies of mask template on page 77 (one per child), copied on to card, coloured pencils, hole punch, shirring elastic.

Cut out the mask and colour in. Punch holes in the sides. Thread with shirring elastic and size to fit the child's head.

Rainbow headband

You will need:
Photocopies of rainbow headband template on page 79 (one per child), copied on to card, photocopies of animal templates on page 78, coloured pencils, scissors, PVA glue or sticky tape.

Help the children to make their own 'Noah's ark' rainbow headbands. Colour in the rainbow. Then choose an animal, colour it in, write the child's name in the square, cut it out and stick it in the middle of the rainbow. Cut out the headband and the extra strips of card, shape the band round the child's head, and stick in place 'made to measure'. You could use the headbands to play games, such as those suggested below.

Who am I?

Collect up all the headbands and then, without revealing which animal is on the front of the band, put one band on each child's head. The children then have to ask questions of each other to find out what sort of animal they have on their band. For example, 'Is it a big animal? Is it small? Would it eat me?' and so on. When the children think they know what animal is on their headband, they ask the leader if they are correct. If they are, they sit down until everyone has discovered which animal they are. To finish the game, you could ask the children to make the noise of the animal on their headband—all together and very loudly.

Happy animals

Make sure every child has a headband on their head. The children then have to find other children with the same animal. The team that finds all their animals first wins.

Razzamatazz calendars

You will need:
Photocopies of the calendar template on page 80 (one per child), photocopied on to mediumweight card, coloured pencils, stick-on calendar pads (available from stationery suppliers), sticky tape, ribbon.

Ask the children to personalize their calendars by creating a picture of God's wonderful creation or a robot scene in the space provided. Stick a calendar pad underneath. Attach a loop of ribbon to the centre top area at the back of the calendar, so that the calendar can be hung up.

Team craft: Junk robots

You will need:
Junk items (cardboard boxes, yoghurt pots, cardboard tubes, bottle tops and so on), tin foil, craft foam, scissors, PVA glue, card, coloured pencils, pipe cleaners, split-pin fasteners.

Put the children into their teams and ask them to design and build a robot using junk items. When the robots are finished, they could be judged for the best design. The children can name their robots and the models can be used as part of the overall display for the holiday club venue.

Prayer chooser

You will need:
Photocopies of prayer chooser template on page 81 (one per child), coloured pencils.

Colour in the prayer chooser and fold as follows.

1. Fold in half across the diagonal. Open out.
2. Fold in half across the other diagonal. Open out.
3. Fold all four corners to centre and crease to flatten.
4. Turn over.
5. Repeat step 3.
6. Fold in half widthways. Press flat. Open out.
7. Repeat step 6 along other width.
8. Slip thumb and forefinger into flaps and form chooser so that it can be opened and closed in both directions.

Team craft: Creation appreciation!

You will need:
Junk items (such as cereal boxes, yoghurt pots, cardboard tubes, newspaper and so on), tissue paper, craft foam, coloured card, scissors, PVA glue, card, A3 paper, coloured pencils, poster paints, brushes, kitchen paper.

With the children in their teams, ask them to design a storyboard model of the seven days of creation. When the models are finished, have a discussion about what we do to look after our beautiful world. Encourage suggestions such as picking up litter, planting trees, saving fuel and so on. Next, give each team a sheet of A3 paper and ask them to design a poster to encourage people to take care of the environment. If desired, the posters could be judged and a small prize given to the winners.

Razzamatazz games

Rampaging robots

Mark out a playing area, inside which the children will move around. In the middle of the playing area, use chairs, benches or tape to mark out the rampaging robots' den.

Choose two children to be the rampaging robots. They go inside the den and all the other children spread out in the playing area around the den. Designate a leader to be the caller. He or she calls out different commands, as follows:

- **Running robots**: all the children run around
- **Resting robots**: all the children rest
- **Wobbly robots**: all the children wobble
- **Rusty robots**: all the children freeze
- **Walking robots**: all the children walk

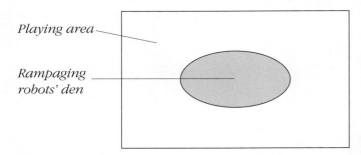

Playing area

Rampaging robots' den

On the command 'Rampaging robots!' the rampaging robots come out of the den and catch as many children as they can in a designated time by tagging them. When caught, the children join the rampaging robots in the den. While in the den, the children who have been caught can continue to follow the commands, but they must remain in the den area. The caller continues to call out the commands. Each time the rampaging robots are called out of the den, more children are caught. The final children left are the winners.

Wobbly robots

This game uses the same set-up as 'Robber robots' (see page 45). Once again, designate a team area for each team around the outside of the playing area and sit the children in a line. Place a box in the middle of each team's area, behind the line of children. Give each child in each team a number, from one to however many children there are in the team.

Place two buckets in the middle of the playing area. Stand the first bucket the right way up and place the second bucket upside down on top of the first. Use sticky-backed paper to give the buckets features and limbs to look like robots. Place a large soft ball in each team's box.

Call out a number. All the children with that number fetch their own team's ball and roll it at the wobbly robot. The ball that reaches the wobbly robot first and knocks it over wins that round. If all the balls miss the robot, there is no score for that round. Continue playing the game, calling out different numbers, until everyone has had a turn. The team with the highest score is the winning team.

Rascal Robot's ravine!

Split the children into two groups. Ask one group to stand on one side of the playing area and the other group on the other side. Choose one person to be Rascal Robot. Rascal Robot stands in the middle of the playing area. This is the robot's ravine. Designate an area to the side of the playing area as Rascal Robot's den.

The aim of the game is for the children to get across to the other side of the playing area by crossing the robot's ravine. The ravine is patrolled by Rascal Robot, the meanest robot ever. Explain that Rascal Robot knows he or she can't catch everyone at once, so the children need to call out, 'Please, Rascal Robot, can we cross the robot ravine?' Rascal Robot replies, 'Only if you're wearing *(name a colour)*, or 'Only if you have *(name a feature such as brown eyes, short hair and so on)*'. Those who meet the criterion walk across safely, watched by Rascal Robot. Then the rest of the children try to cross without being caught by Rascal Robot. Those who are caught sit in Rascal Robot's den until there is a winner.

Robber robots

Put the children into their teams. Designate a team area for each team around the outside of the playing area and sit the children in a line. Place a bucket or box in the middle of each team's area, behind the line of children. Give each child in each team a number, from one to however many children there are in the team. Set out ten 'robots' in the middle of the room. These can be wooden spoons, beanbags or soft balls.

To play the game, call out a number. All the children with that number run to the middle of the room and take *just one* 'robot'. They run back to their team and put the robot into their team's bucket. The same children then run back to the middle to collect another robot.

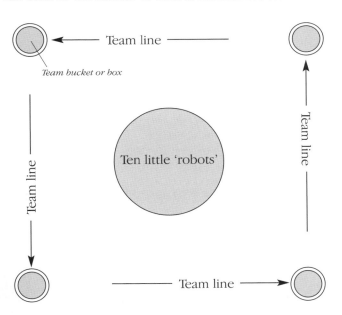

Team bucket or box

Once all the robots have been taken from the middle, they are allowed to take a robot out of another team's bucket. The children in the team from which the child is stealing are not allowed to prevent their robot from being stolen. However, while a child is stealing from another team's bucket, someone else may be stealing from their team's bucket.

The first team to get four robots in their bucket is the winning team. Repeat the game by calling out a new number and so on until all the children have had a turn.

Racing robots relay races

These games aim to test the little robots' special features. Put the children into their teams and line each team up at one end of the playing area. The first child in each team performs the test, travelling to the far end of the playing area and back. The front child then tags the second child, who performs the test, and so on down the lines. The first team to complete the course and have everyone sitting back down in a straight line is the winning team.

Rocket robots

Test your little robots' top speed! Place some cones at the far end of the playing area (one per team). The first child in each team runs to the cone and back, tagging the next child on their return. The next child does the same, and so on until every child has run the course and everyone in the team is sitting down in a straight line. The first team to complete the course is the winning team.

Rolo robots

Test your little robots' nose control! Give each team a mini packet of Rolos. The first child in each team has to use their nose to roll the packet of Rolos down the playing area, around the cone and back again. On their return, the next child takes over and does the same, and so on until every child has completed the course and everyone in the team is sitting down in a straight line. The first team to complete the course is the winning team, but all the teams can share their Rolos when the game is finished. (Have some spare packs to share so that everyone has a Rolo.)

NB: Please be aware of food allergies and use an alternative small packet of sweets that can be rolled in the same way if necessary.

Bouncing robots

Test the strength of your little robots' legs! Give each team a large, heavy-duty bin bag. The first child in each team climbs into the bin bag and jumps to the cone and back, climbing out of the bin bag and tagging the next child on their return. The next child climbs into the bag and does the same, and so on until every child has jumped the course and everyone in the team is sitting down in a straight line. The first team to complete the course is the winning team.

Beanbag balancing robots

Test the steadiness of your little robots! Give each team a beanbag. The first child in each team balances the beanbag on his or her head and walks steadily down the playing area to the cone and back, tagging the next child on their return. The next child takes the beanbag and does the same, and so on until every child has completed the course and everyone in the team is sitting down in a straight line. If a child drops his or her beanbag, they have to run back and start again from the beginning of the line. The first team to complete the course is the winning team.

Remote control robot relay

Set up an obstacle course using cones, tables, benches, chairs, netting, hoops and anything else you might have to hand that can be climbed over, balanced on, climbed through or crawled under. Put the children into their teams and line up the teams at one end of the playing area. Blindfold the child at the front of each team line.

The second child in each team line has to direct and instruct the blindfolded team member down the course, pretending that they are moving the blindfolded player with a remote control. Once the blindfolded player gets to the end of the line, the two players swap roles and come back up the obstacle course. The next two children in the team's line then go down the course in the same manner. The first team to get all the team members up the course and back is the winning team.

The animals went in two by two

The animals are often depicted going into Noah's ark in a very calm manner, but I wonder if, in reality, anxious at the thought of all that rain on the way, they might have hurried in in a less orderly fashion.

Put the children into their teams. Designate a team area for each team around the outside of the playing area and sit the children in a line. Give each child in each team a number, from one to however many children there are in the team. Have two balls or beanbags in the centre of the playing area to represent the ark.

Call out one or two numbers and an animal name (see list below)—for example, 'One and seven and an elephant'. If two numbers are called, the children with the first number called become the front of the animal and the children with the second number become the back of the animal. The pairs of players get into position and then run (or move like the animal) as quickly as possible to the balls. The first two players to pick up the balls or beanbags have arrived at the ark and win points for their team. If the animals come apart in the middle, then they have to go back to the start.

Animals

- **Elephant:** Call two numbers. The front person stands upright and raises their arm to represent a trunk as they run. The back person bends down and holds the waist of the person in front.
- **Giraffe:** Call two numbers. The front person stands upright and lifts their arms high to represent the giraffe's neck, forming the head with their hands. The back person bends down and holds the waist of the person in front.
- **Kangaroo:** Call one number. The players have to jump all the way to the middle.
- **Crab:** Call one number. The players have to move sideways on all fours.
- **Gorilla:** Call one number. The players have to run while hitting their chest and making gorilla noises.
- **Lion:** Call one number. The players have to run on all fours, roaring as they go.
- **Flamingo:** Call one number. The players have to stand on one leg and hop all the way to the middle.

Animal run around

Choose four or five people to hold a picture card of an animal. The card holders need to space out around the outside of the room. All the children run around the room. On a given signal, such as blowing a whistle, all the children choose an animal by lining up in front of the person holding the picture of that animal.

Have a bag with the same animal cards inside. When everyone has chosen an animal, take an animal card out of the bag. All the children who have chosen the same animal as the one on the card are out. Continue playing until only one child is left in the game. This child is the winner and scores a point for his or her team. Repeat the game until you run out of time or energy.

NB: When only a few children are left in the game, encourage them to choose different animals rather than following each other.

Razzamatazz robot ladders

Split the children into two groups. Form two lines, so every child stands opposite a child from the other group. Ask the children to take off their shoes and place them (in a line) at the edge of the playing area. When the children are ready, put them back into their two lines. Space the two lines so that the children are an arm's length apart and still opposite the child from the other group. (If there are a lot of children, form two double rows.)

Ask the children to sit down facing the child from the opposite team. They then need to stretch out their legs so that their feet are touching the feet of the child opposite. Go down the line and give each pair of children (one from each group) one of the following character names. If you have more than ten children in the line, keep naming the children from the top of the character name list until everyone has been given a name.

Read the story below very slowly. Every time the children hear their character's name, they stand up and step out of the line. They then run to the front of the line (round the outside) and back down the middle of the line, taking care not to step on any legs as they come down the 'ladder'. Once they have completed running down the ladder, they run round the back of the line and back to their place. Carry on reading the story very slowly, giving the children time to return if they are called out in quick succession, but also ensuring that there are always children running.

Grandma Watt is a clever little old lady. So, when **Rick** and **Wendy** wanted a **robot** of their own, she decided they could build one. After many hours of hard work, the Watt family had finally finished their **robot**. They called him **Ro Botwatt**.

Unfortunately, **Ro Botwatt** didn't work quite as well as **Grandma**, **Rick** and **Wendy** had planned. First of all, he dropped eggs all over the floor. Then he went into a spin. **Rick** and **Wendy** were not impressed. Soon there were eggs and flour everywhere. What a mess! **Professor Rolo's robots** would never behave as badly as **Ro Botwatt**! **Rick** and **Wendy** pleaded with **Grandma** to let them go to **Professor Rolo's** shop and talk to the **shop assistant**.

Finally, **Grandma** agreed and, leaving **Ro Botwatt** at home, off they went. The **shop assistant** was very pleased to see the Watt family. He was very enthusiastic about **Professor Rolo's** fantastic Razzamatazz Robots. First of all, he introduced them to the URACM, which stands for 'You are a cake maker'. That **robot** was very impressive. Next, he brought out the URAGP, which stands for 'You are a games player'. **Rick** and **Wendy** were very impressed. Next, he showed them the URAWC, which stands for 'You are a window cleaner'. Last, but by no means least, the **shop assistant** brought out the

URAHD, which stands for 'You are a hairdresser'. **Grandma** was not impressed with that one. Which **robot** would the Watt family choose? The **shop assistant** tried to make them buy all four by giving them a special offer: buy three, get one free! **Rick** and **Wendy** thought this was very good, but **Grandma** Watt wasn't so sure.

Just at that moment, who should walk through the door but **Professor Rolo** himself! The **shop assistant** nearly fainted. **Professor Rolo** was working on his next invention—a superduper **robot** that would be the best of all. The Watt family's homemade **Ro Botwatt** could never compete with this. The URACD was so clever that they decided to call him **Albert**, after Einstein, who was also very clever. **Albert** was a cool mover; he could spin round and even do tricks. Even **Grandma** was impressed by **Albert's** cleverness.

Professor Rolo and the **shop assistant** were delighted that **Rick** and **Wendy** had persuaded **Grandma** to buy **Albert**. He was the coolest **robot** they had ever seen. No wonder **Professor Rolo** had given him the name URACD, which stands for 'You are a cool dude'! Well done, **Albert**! But, however impressive **Albert** is, perhaps our most favourite is still the Watt family's very own homemade **Ro Botwatt**.

Puppet sketches

Day One: Creation appreciation!

Bert and Lucy come up, arguing.

Lucy: You never appreciate anything, Bert!

Bert: I do! I appreciated you coming round the other day.

Lucy: Of course you did. I brought (*latest Game Boy game*) with me, that's why!

Bert: I'm sorry, Lucy, but we really shouldn't be arguing. We haven't said 'hello' to these guys yet and that's very bad manners. *(Both look at audience)*

Bert and Lucy: Hi, everyone!

Lucy: Sorry if I sound a bit stressed, it's just that Bert asked me out on a date…

Bert: *(Interrupting)* It wasn't a date!

Lucy: … to the school disco—and then he wouldn't dance with me.

Bert: Dancing isn't really my thing.

Lucy: He didn't mention how beautiful I looked.

Bert: What?

Lucy: I was wearing my brand new, very cool and very pretty party dress especially for you, and you didn't even notice.

Bert: Of course I did!

Lucy: I went to all that effort to look nice for you. I washed and brushed my hair. Mum even let me wear my clip-on earrings. I even wore perfume.

Bert: Oh, I wondered what that funny smell was.

Lucy: And you didn't even notice.

Bert: I did!

Lucy: Not even one little compliment.

Bert: I did notice!

Lucy: OK, how did I have my hair, then?

Bert: In a bun.

Lucy: No! What did my earrings look like?

Bert: Er… pretty, I think.

Lucy: Were they hoop earrings, drop earrings, pear shape, stud, silver, or gold? You haven't got a clue!

Bert: Er, no, but it was a pretty dress, though.

Lucy: Ha! Who are you trying to kid? You never even noticed it!

Bert: I did!

Lucy: What colour was it? Was it long or short?

Bert: Pink.

Lucy: No!

Bert: Pink with green spots?

Lucy: No, no, no!

Bert: Green with pink spots?

Lucy: Bert, it's not funny. You're a typical boy! I spent ages trying to look nice and you didn't even notice. You don't appreciate me at all.

Bert: I'm sorry, Lucy, if I took your beauty for granted.

Lucy: *(Amazed)* Took my beauty for granted? Oh Bert, that's the nicest thing you've ever said to me! *(She gives him a big kiss and leaves)*

Bert: *(To audience)* Er… what did I say? *(Pause)* Anyway, looks like we're off—but I've learnt my lesson. Appreciate Lucy more—or suffer eternal nagging! Bye everyone, bye!

Day Two: Creation's crown!

Lucy:	*(Comes up a little upset)* She didn't want me!
Bert:	*(Comes up)* Who didn't want you?
Lucy:	*(A little louder with sobs)* She didn't want me!
Bert:	Gosh, Lucy, you're really upset! What's up?
Lucy:	*(Sobs)* My best friend Sarah Jane didn't invite me to her sleepover. It's not fair; she didn't want me.
Bert:	Oh right, yeah, that's not very fair. Is it because you snore?
Lucy:	*(Looks crossly at Bert)* I do not snore! *(Quietly)* Do I?
Bert:	No, I'm sure you don't. Perhaps she can only invite a few friends and she's planning to invite you to something else.
Lucy:	No, she lives in a huge house and has a bedroom bigger than my house. Perhaps that's it—she doesn't think I'm good enough for her.
Bert:	I'm sure that's not right.
Lucy:	It must be right. It all makes sense now. She went on a camping holiday with some friends, but guess who wasn't invited again?
Bert:	No idea.
Lucy:	Me! That's who! Why didn't she invite me? Do I smell?
Bert:	Of course you do!
Lucy:	*(Looking concerned)* What? Really?
Bert:	Yes! We all smell with our noses. That was my little joke.
Lucy:	Well, it's not funny. I'm trying to be all upset and emotional here.
Bert:	Sorry, of course you don't smell. I would politely tell you if you did. I'd say something like, 'Cor, you stink!'
Lucy:	You call that polite? *(She looks sad again)* But I still don't understand. She went to the fair the other day with her friends and told me about it afterwards. Am I boring company? Perhaps they think I'm ugly and they don't want to be seen with me. Am I not worth bothering with? After all, I haven't been chosen for the school football team. I'm never going to get ten out of ten in tests at school, even though I try really hard. I'm just useless!
Bert:	No, you're not, Lucy! You're fantastic and my best friend. You're a good laugh; you're kind and clever, too. And I think you're… *(whispering with embarrassment)* really pretty.
Lucy:	Oh Bert, I think you're the best, too.
Bert:	Look, Lucy, if Sarah Jane and her friends don't want you around, then they're the ones who are missing out. But who is this Sarah Jane? I don't think I know her.
Lucy:	She's my pen pal. She lives in America.
Bert:	What? Of course she doesn't invi…
Lucy:	*(Interrupting)* Come on, Bert, you've made my day! I am special after all. Bye, everyone!
Bert:	Yeah, bye!

Day Three: Careless whispers!

Lucy:	Hi there, everyone! Has anyone seen my Bert? I'm a bit surprised that he's not here. He did sound a bit sad on the phone earlier. I hope he's OK. *(She calls out)* Oh Bert! Bert…

Bert appears, looking sad.

Lucy:	What's the matter, Bert? You look really sad. What's up, mate?
Bert:	I made a chocolate cake.
Lucy:	*(Surprised)* Ha, you made a chocolate cake?
Bert:	Yes. It was wonderful! I made a yummy sponge cake and covered it in thick chocolate spread, then I got about 100 candles and I was about to put them on. It took me ages and ages to make and bake.
Lucy:	It sounds fantastic. Can I have a slice?
Bert:	No! Someone's ruined it.
Lucy:	Ruined it? Let me at them! No one ruins my friend's chocolate cake and gets away with it. What happened?
Bert:	Well, as I said, it took me ages and ages to make and bake. It's my mum's birthday. I think she's 100 years old—at least, that's what Dad says. Chocolate cake is her favourite, so I thought I would make her one for her birthday cake.
Lucy:	Yummy, it's my favourite, too.
Bert:	I can see that. It looks like you've got some chocolate round your mouth.
Lucy:	Yummy, yes, I probably have. *(Bert looks very upset; he's not really listening)* You wouldn't believe it—I walked into the kitchen at church and I thought I was in heaven. There on the side was a chocolate cake. I'm afraid temptation got the better of me.

Bert:	*(Looks up)* Sorry, Lucy, what did you say? I wasn't really listening. You see, I had to make my chocolate cake in the kitchen at church so my mum wouldn't come in while I was making it. *(Lucy starts to shake)* Are you all right, Lucy? You're shaking and you've gone a little pale.
Lucy:	Er-r-r! I'm fine, really!
Bert:	Anyway, where was I? I finally finished the cake and went to get the candles, but when I came back someone had cut a huge slice and eaten it. There were crumbs everywhere.
Lucy:	It was only a little slice.
Bert:	Pardon?
Lucy:	Er… nothing! Let's say goodbye, shall we?
Bert:	No! I don't want to go! What do you mean, it was only a little slice?
Lucy:	*(Shaking violently now)* I didn't know it was your mum's birthday cake.
Bert:	IT WAS YOU!
Lucy:	Yes, but it was only a little slice.
Bert:	BIG!
Lucy:	Little!
Bert:	Whatever made you cut a big slice out of my cake?
Lucy:	I didn't know it was yours. When I saw it, I thought, 'The Lord provides' and I was hungry, so I tucked in.
Bert:	How could you?
Lucy:	I'm really, really, really sorry, Bert.
Bert:	Too late! The damage is done.
Lucy:	Yes, I can see that. I know. Let's make another one. I'll buy all the ingredients and we can make it together, eating your first cake to keep us going.
Bert:	Oh, I suppose so.
Lucy:	Bye, everyone, we've got a cake to make.
Bert:	Bye!

Day Four: Enough's enough!

Lucy:	Hi, everyone! I'm really excited because it's arrived, it's finally arrived!
Bert:	What's arrived? Is it a baby?
Lucy:	No! And you know exactly what I mean. My go-cart! Dad always talks about the go-cart he had as a boy—his was made with wood and old pram wheels.
Bert:	What's a pram?
Lucy:	It's a bit like an old-fashioned pushchair for babies. When his pram was old and no good to put babies in, his dad—my grandad—took the wheels off the pram and, by using some wood, made a go-
	cart. My dad and grandad had loads of fun on it.
Bert:	So you wanted one, too?
Lucy:	I sure did. We found a 'build it yourself' go-cart on the Internet. It includes the wood and the front and back wheels, the string, all the fasteners, everything. I can't wait to build it.
Bert:	You don't have to. Before holiday club *(or service)* I went to your house, but no one was there. Then I saw the box with go-cart bits in your shed. So I thought, seeing as you're my best friend and a girl—we men are always better at building things, so I put it together for you. I've even got the paint ready to paint it for you.
Lucy:	*(Opened mouthed)* But, but, Bert, I was looking forward to building it.
Bert:	Well, that's gratitude for you! I did it because you are my friend.
Lucy:	*(Hears a phone ringing)* That's the phone. I'd better answer it. *(She disappears)*
Bert:	*(To audience)* I have been kind, haven't I?
Lucy:	*(Reappears looking cross)* That was my dad. He's seen the go-cart. Did you read the instructions about how to build it?
Bert:	Of course not. We men don't need instructions.
Lucy:	Bert, you've put one back wheel on the front—*(to audience)* the back wheels are bigger than the front ones—*(to Bert)* and one front wheel on the back. You've put the seat on the bottom of the go-cart. Do you expect me to sit upside down? And the cord to pull it along with is all tangled up.
Bert:	Apart from that, is it all right?
Lucy:	*(Shouts)* No, it's not all right! And on top of all that, you've opened a can of pink paint. I don't want a pink go-cart. You didn't follow the instructions and now you've ruined it. I'm going to have to start all over again.
Bert:	*(Looking guilty)* Oops! Sorry, Lucy. Can you forgive me, like I forgave you yesterday for ruining my mum's birthday cake?
Lucy:	Oh, yeah. I suppose so. But we're going to have to start all over again. And this time, Dad is going to help and I'll make sure we follow the maker's instructions. Otherwise it will end up in a mess again.
Bert:	Good idea! We'd better go. Bye!
Lucy:	Bye, everyone!

Day Five: The Master's plan

Lucy: I almost made a terrible mistake the other day.

Bert: How come?

Lucy: I saw my friend Charlie and he had just come back from America with the most incredible toy robot ever. This robot could sort of talk, pick things up, throw things, give you a high five, whistle, dance and do karate moves.

Bert: Wow! Sounds fantastic!

Lucy: It is.

Bert: Wow, I would love a robot like that.

Lucy: That's what *I* said. And Charlie said something amazing.

Bert: What?

Lucy: He said he'd swap it for chewing gum.

Bert: Chewing gum?

Lucy: Yeah! So I said 'Done!' and got out my last piece of chewing gum and went to swap it, but he said, 'Not that chewing gum!' The only other piece I had, I was chewing in my mouth, so I went to take it out of my mouth, but he said…

Bert: *(Interrupting)* Yuck!

Lucy: Yeah, that's exactly what he said, and then he said, 'Not that chewing gum' again.

Bert: What, then?

Lucy: You mean 'Who'.

Bert: Oh no, he doesn't mean your guinea pig, does he?

Lucy: Exactly. Chewing Gum is the name of my guinea pig.

Bert: I hope you said 'No way'. You've had Chewing Gum for years.

Lucy: Yeah, but can Chewing Gum talk?

Bert: Well, not in human language, no.

Lucy: Can Chewing Gum whistle or give high fives or do cool dance moves or karate moves?

Bert: Well, no! But you do say that Chewing Gum is your best friend—apart from me, of course.

Lucy: Charlie's robot cost a lot more money than Chewing Gum. I could never afford a robot like that.

Bert: Yes, but…

Lucy: His robot doesn't wee on people he doesn't like. You wouldn't have to clean out the robot's hutch, because he wouldn't need one. Plus, you don't have to feed him.

Bert: What about batteries?

Lucy: Don't be silly, Bert, guinea pigs don't have batteries.

Bert: No, I meant the robot! You said 'Yes', didn't you?

Lucy: Of course I did! I was getting a bargain. I took Chewing Gum out of her hutch and went to swap her, but then she looked at me with those cute eyes and started her sweet squeaking. I stroked her soft fur and looked at her one last time with her little cute legs, big fat body, sharp claws and cute ears. I couldn't do it.

Bert: What?

Lucy: I couldn't make the swap. She might not be as clever as the robot in being able to do tricks, but she's much better at cuddles and cheering me up when I'm a bit sad.

Bert: Yes. She's your friend, and friends are always better than things!

Lucy: Yeah, I did make the right decision, didn't I? Bye, everyone!

Bert: Bye!

 Reproduced with permission from *Razzamatazz Robots Holiday Club!* published by BRF 2008 (978 1 84101 577 4)

Quick quiz questions

Quizzes are a wonderful way to recap what the children have learnt and a good opportunity for the children to earn points for their team. Some of the quick quiz questions below are about the Bible story and Bible memory verses, some about the Watt family or Bert and Lucy, and some are general knowledge and just for fun. Where an answer needs a description rather than a single-word reply, allow some flexibility in the answers. The questions are age-banded as follows:

- Question 1 is for the youngest group.
- Question 2 is for the middle group.
- Question 3 is for the older group.
- Question 4 is an extra question if needed.

Day One: Creation appreciation!

Odd one out

1. Little Robots, Bob the Builder, The News, The Tweenies
   (The News)
2. Power Rangers, Sugar Babes, Daleks, Teenage Mutant Turtles
   (Sugar Babes)
3. R2D2, K9, Data, Bruno
   (Bruno: he was a boxer)
4. Vacuum cleaner, computer, microwave, teddy
   (Teddy)

Bert and Lucy and the Watt family

1. In the puppet sketch, why was Lucy cross with Bert?
   (He didn't appreciate her)

2. The Watt family tried to build their own robot, but what happened?
   (It didn't work properly)
3. Who invented the Razzamatazz Robots?
   (Professor Rolo)
4. Why didn't Grandma like the Professor's robots?
   (They all looked the same / she didn't like the words in the slogan)

General Bible

1. Who did David fight: a robot, a spaceman, a giant named Goliath or a crocodile?
   (A giant named Goliath)
2. What sort of animal did Jesus ride on: an elephant, a kangaroo, a donkey or a giraffe?
   (A donkey)
3. In the story of the feeding of the 5000, what did the boy have in his lunch: five lollipops and two chocolates, two loaves and five fishes, two burgers and five chips or five loaves and two fishes?
   (Five loaves and two fishes)
4. What sort of book is the Bible: a maths book, a cookery book, God's special book or a dictionary?
   (God's special book)

Day Two: Creation's crown!

Bert and Lucy and the Watt family

1. In the puppet sketch, why didn't Lucy's friend Sarah Jane invite her to things?
   (She lives in America)

2. Yesterday, what couldn't the Watt family's robot pick up without breaking it?
   (An egg)
3. Name some of the jobs the UR robot series could do.
   (Cake maker, games player, window cleaner, hairdresser)
4. Why is the superduper URACD robot so special?
   (It can do all the household chores)

General knowledge

1. Which name isn't from *Little Robots*: Tiny, Sporty, Scary, Rusty or Gromit?
   (Gromit)
2. Name something that makes people so special.
   (Caring, creative, think for themselves and so on)
3. Name something that a robot can't do.
   (Share a joke, have a chat and so on)
4. Ask the team to sing yesterday's memory verse.
   (Genesis, chapter one, verse 31: It was good, it was very, very good!)

Bible story

1. In yesterday's Bible story, who made the world?
   (God)
2. What was it like at the very beginning of creation?
   (Dark)
3. Name some of the things that God made in the story of creation.
   (Light, vegetation, animals, sun, water, moon, fish, birds and so on)
4. What was the last and the most special thing God made?
   (People)

Day Three: Careless whispers!

Bert and Lucy and the Watt family

1. In today's puppet sketch, who did Bert made a birthday cake for?
   (His mum)
2. Who ruined the cake by eating a huge slice?
   (Lucy)
3. What did the Watt family call their Razzamatazz Robot?
   (Albert)
4. Why did the Watt family allow Albert to stay in bed?
   (It was his birthday)

General Bible and memory verses

1. Which is the first book of the Bible?
   (Genesis)
2. What are the four Gospels called?
   (Matthew, Mark, Luke and John)
3. As a team, sing yesterday's Bible memory verse.
   (Psalm 139, verse 14: I will praise you)
4. As a team, sing today's Bible memory verse.
   (Proverbs 3, verse 6: Remember, remember the Lord)

Bible story

1. What is the name of the first man?
   (Adam)
2. Why was Adam lonely?
   (There was no one else like him)
3. What is the name of the first woman?
   (Eve)
4. What is the name of the garden in which Adam and Eve lived?
   (The garden of Eden)

Day Four: Enough's enough!

Bert and Lucy and the Watt family

1. In today's puppet sketch, what had arrived that made Lucy so excited?
   (Her go-cart kit)
2. What did Bert do that made him so unpopular with Lucy?
   (He tried to build her go-cart, but didn't follow the instructions)
3. In the Watt family drama, who came to the rescue when Professor Rolo lost the plot and captured Grandma and Rick?
   (Wendy)
4. What will Professor Rolo's satellites do to the robots?
   (Send them a message to capture people everywhere)

Bible memory verses

1. Ask for a volunteer or a whole team to sing a memory verse.
2. Ask for another volunteer from the next team to sing a different memory verse.
3. Ask the third team or a volunteer to sing a different memory verse.
4. Sing today's memory verse.

Bible story

1. In yesterday's Bible story, what did God tell Adam and Eve not to eat?
   (The fruit from his special tree)
2. Who came along to tempt Eve? Did she eat the fruit?
   (A snake; yes, she did)
3. Why was God upset with Adam and Eve?
   (Because they had disobeyed him and couldn't be trusted)
4. Who does the snake in the story represent?
   (The devil / Satan)

Day Five: The Master's plan

Bert and Lucy and the Watt family

1. In today's puppet sketch, what was the name of Lucy's guinea pig?
   (Chewing Gum)
2. Why wouldn't Lucy swap her guinea pig for the cool toy robot?
   (Chewing Gum was her best friend)
3. In today's Watt family drama, what did Professor Rolo discover about robots?
   (They can never really replace humans)
4. At the end of the drama, why didn't Professor Rolo carry out his really mean, dishonest and dastardly plan?
   (The Watt family became his friends and trusted him)

Bible memory verses

1. As a team, sing a memory verse.
2. As a team, sing a different memory verse.
3. As a team, sing another memory verse.
4. And another!

Bible story

1. In yesterday's Bible story, who did God tell to build an ark?
   (Noah)
2. Why did God plan to flood the earth?
   (People had become so evil)
3. Apart from Noah and his family, what else did God save?
   (Two of every kind of animal)
4. When God promised never to destroy the earth again, what sign did he send to show us how much he loves us?
   (A rainbow)

Bible story narrations

Day One: Creation appreciation!

Bible story: Genesis 1:1–25

> **Cast**
> Narrator and two others (A and B)
>
> **Props**
> Creation images on PowerPoint (optional), sign cards for the days of creation (see script), a water pistol, a bucket filled with torn-up pieces of paper

Narrator: In the beginning…

A: *(Interrupts)* Hey, *(name of narrator)*, were you there at the beginning?

B: Beginning of what?

A: The universe! The beginning of the world!

B: *(Seriously)* Good question, *(name of A)*. *(To narrator)* Yeah, were you there?

Narrator: Watch it, you guys! Are you trying to say I'm old? But to answer your question, no one was there apart from God.

A: So no one knows exactly how the earth was created, then?

B: And no one knows exactly how you make water or animals or humans or trees or…

Narrator: *(Interrupts)* That's exactly right. We try to understand how the world began based on the evidence people have found. But the only one who really knows for sure is…

All: GOD!

Narrator: There is a story about how the world began in the first book of the Bible—the book of Genesis, which means 'beginning'.

Narrator reads slowly, giving A and B time to act out the story and throw in a few comments without losing the flow. A PowerPoint presentation of images to accompany the story could also be used. A and B hold up a sign saying: The first day…

Narrator: In the beginning it was very dark…

A and B put their hands over their eyes.

A and B: Dark! Dark! Very dark!

Narrator: The earth was under a raging ocean…

B: Water, water everywhere!

A and B pretend to swim in the dark, with their eyes closed.

Narrator: And then God said, 'Let there be light!'

A and B open their eyes on the word 'light', but continue to swim.

A: Ah, that's better.

B: Now I can see.

Narrator: God called the light 'day'…

A and B look impressed—they are still swimming.

Narrator: … and the dark he called 'night'.

A and B yawn and snore—still swimming.

Narrator: And God saw that the light was good.

A: Hey, that's all right! *(Gives a thumbs up)*

Narrator: Evening came… and then morning.

 Reproduced with permission from *Razzamatazz Robots Holiday Club!* published by BRF 2008 (978 1 84101 577 4)

A and B stop swimming and hold up a sign saying: The second day...

Narrator: ...so God separated the water...

A: Sounds good to me!

B gives a thumbs up.

Narrator: ...and named the waters above the earth 'sky'.

B: Is that a rain cloud I see?

A shoots water from a water pistol into the air over the audience.

Narrator: Evening came... and then morning.

A and B hold up a sign saying: The third day...

Narrator: Then God said, 'Let the water below the sky come together in one place...'

A and B look down at the ground and jump in unison.

A and B: Solid!

Narrator: God named the dry ground 'land'...

A and B nod and look impressed.

Narrator: ...and the water he named 'sea'.

B picks up the bucket and pretends to throw water over the audience.

Narrator: And God looked at what he had done and saw that it was good.

A: Hey, that's all right! *(Gives a thumbs up)*

Narrator: Then God said, 'Let the earth produce plants, fruit trees and grain.'

A: Yeah, we need vegetation!

B: Plants!

A grows like a plant.

A: Trees!

B stands rigid like a tree.

B: Seeds!

A mimes right hand picking up a tiny seed from palm of left hand.

A: Fruit!

B mimes taking a bite from an apple.

B: Yummy!

Narrator: Evening came... and then morning.

A and B hold up a sign saying: The fourth day...

Narrator: And then God said, 'Let two lights appear in the sky to separate day from night and show the times and seasons.'

A: Good idea! Plants need heat and light to grow.

Narrator: The sun to light the day...

B: Phew! It's warm!

A and B fan themselves.

Narrator: ... and the moon to light the night. And he also made the stars.

A and B both point up to different places, nodding and looking most impressed.

A: Wow! What an excellent sight!

Narrator: Evening came... and then morning.

A and B hold up a sign saying: The fifth day...

Narrator: God said, 'Let the sea be full of living creatures...'

B swims across stage like a fish or shark.

Narrator: '... and let the sky be filled with birds.'

A flies across stage like a bird.

Narrator: And God looked at what he had done and saw that it was good.

B: Hey, that's all right! *(Gives a thumbs up)*

Narrator: Evening came... and then morning.

A and B hold up a sign saying: The sixth day...

Narrator: God said, 'Let all kinds of creatures live on the land.'

B: Animals everywhere!

A and B act like monkeys.

Narrator: Did you know that there are about 600 varieties of spider in the UK?

B: Aaarrgh! *(Jumps into A's arms. They both look scared)*

Narrator: God made every one of them.

B: Oh, that's all right, then. *(They both calm down)*

Narrator:	And God looked at what he had done and saw that it was good.
A:	Brilliant world, God! *(Gives a thumbs up)*
B:	Yeah, you've thought of everything!
Narrator:	Not quite! Just one more to create… *(pause)* And then God made human beings.

A and B proudly point to themselves.

| Narrator: | God made people to be like himself. |
| A: | Great—now we can relate. |

A puts hands together in the gesture of a prayer; B mimes just chatting.

| Narrator: | God put human beings in charge of everything in creation. |

Narrator looks at A and B. A and B nod.

Narrator:	God looked at what he had done and saw that it was very good.
A:	Hey, I'm really looking forward to getting to know God.
Narrator:	And God is looking forward to getting to know you.
B:	But first we need a rest.

A and B hold up a sign saying: The seventh day…

Narrator:	And that's just what God did! On the seventh day, he rested. Everything had been carefully created and everything fitted together. God made the seventh day special because that was the day he rested from his work.
A:	Is that the end of our story?
Narrator:	It's the end and it's the beginning.
A:	Fantastic!
B:	Awesome!
A:	Incredible!
B:	Stupendous!
Narrator:	Yes, just a few words to describe God and the wonderful world he made for us to enjoy. Well done, guys!

All take a bow.

Bible story: Genesis 1:26–31; Genesis 2:4b–25; Psalm 8:5

Cast
Narrator and two others (A and B)

Narrator:	Wow! Can you imagine what it must have been like to be the first person God ever created? You would have had the whole world all to yourself.
A:	Sounds fantastic!
Narrator:	Just you and all the animals They were all friendly in those days.
B:	Didn't they live in a special garden?
Narrator:	Yes, God made a special garden that he called the garden of Eden. Wow, it was a brilliant place—full of beautiful trees with amazing leaves and fruit, a stream to relax by, the song of birds filling the air and the company of all the animals.
A:	Sounds like heaven!
Narrator:	God asked the first person to look after everything he had made.
B:	Uh-oh! Big mistake!
Narrator:	Not at all! You see, God made human beings in his image, which means we can think things through and work things out. We can create and invent things, just like God does. God didn't make us to be like robots; he made us so that we can make our own choices and think for ourselves. We are amazing! *(To A and B)* You are amazing!
A and B:	Thank you very much!
Narrator:	Your eyes are amazing.
A:	Good for seeing with.
Narrator:	Your ears are amazing.
B:	Good for hearing with.
Narrator:	Your hands are brilliant.
A:	Good for making things with.
Narrator:	In fact, your whole body is wonderfully made!
B:	*(Dances around)* Why, thank you, thank you, kind sir—you're not so bad yourself!
Narrator:	And you are one of a kind. You are unique. You haven't come off a factory production line—you have been carefully designed by the creator of the world.
B:	What a fantastic God!
Narrator:	*(Looks at A)* And as for your brain…
A:	Watch it!
Narrator:	… there is nothing in the universe to match it.
A:	Thank you!

Narrator:	Your brain is continually absorbing information.
B:	What does that mean?
A:	*(To B)* It means you are continually learning new things.
Narrator:	Your brain is continually producing new ideas… I could go on all day.
A:	Please do!
Narrator:	No time for that! Let's get back to the story. God named the first person 'Adam', which means 'man'. The Bible tells us that God actually used to walk in the garden with Adam.
B:	*(Excitedly)* Wow! How cool is that! I wonder what sort of things they used to chat about.
Narrator:	Perhaps God said something like…
B:	Adam, what do you think of the garden? Do you like the trees and the fruit?
Narrator:	Perhaps Adam replied…
A:	Oh yeah! The garden is fantastic, the trees are solid and strong, and the fruit is juicy and sweet. And, wow, water is incredible—you can see right through it and it's brilliant to cool off in. And then there are fish of every colour, so many different birds and animals of every shape and size…
Narrator:	And perhaps God smiled, because he knew that everything was good. It was very, very good.
A:	*(Thoughtfully)* Yeah, I've never really thought about it before. There is a huge amount of variety, isn't there? Our world really is an awesome place.

B gives a big sigh.

A:	What's the matter with you? I thought everything was perfect.
B:	Well, yes… but have you ever tried to chat with a giraffe? You get a stiff neck after a while. Have you ever tried to share a meal with a lion? One bite and he has eaten the lot. Have you ever shared a joke with a hyena? He's laughing before you get to the punch line. Have you ever had a jog with a leopard, or shared a bath with a hippo? The fact is, it's a bit lonely being the only human being in the world.
A:	I see what you mean. You're lonely. You need a companion.
Narrator:	So while Adam was sleeping, God got to work… and when Adam woke up he couldn't believe his eyes.
B:	*(To A)* Wow! *(Whistles)* What a babe! Who is this ravishing creature?
Narrator:	This, Adam, is Eve. I hope you two will be

	very happy together.
B:	*(Excitedly)* Boy, am I pleased to meet you!
Narrator:	From that day, Adam, Eve and God enjoyed the garden together. Everything was just as God intended it to be—perfect, just perfect.

A and B exit arm in arm.

Narrator:	Or was it…? *(Exits)*

Day Three: Careless whispers!

Bible story: Genesis 3:1–8

Cast
Narrator and two others (A and B)

Props
A sock snake puppet (optional)

Narrator:	Life couldn't have been better for Adam and Eve. They had each other to talk to, and all the beautiful, friendly animals to enjoy. The garden was paradise. Fantastic! They often used to walk with God in the garden, chatting and enjoying each other's company.
A:	Sounds perfect!
Narrator:	It was! There was just one thing that they were not allowed to do. There was a tree in the middle of the garden, which was God's special tree and they were not allowed to eat its fruit.
B:	No problem!
A:	We've got loads of other trees to pick fruit from.
Narrator:	And they meant it. They really were quite happy without going near God's special tree. *(Pause)* But one day Eve was walking along… *(A mimes walking)* when suddenly…

B hisses loudly, like a snake. A looks round but doesn't see anything, so shrugs shoulders and carries on walking. B hisses even louder. A looks round again.

B:	*(Slyly)* Thisss way… I'm over here!

B makes a snake shape with his/her arm. You could use a sock puppet at this point.

A:	Aarrgh! A talking snake!
B:	Oh yesss, but not any old sssnake, my dear. Have you ssseen that tree over there?
A:	*(Looks in same direction as the 'snake')* Oh yes, that's God's special tree. We're allowed to eat the fruit from any tree in the garden except that one.
B:	I sssee. And why would that be?
A:	Why would what be?
B:	Why aren't you allowed to eat the fruit from that tree?
A:	Because God said so.
B:	Ha! What doesss he know?
A:	*(Hesitates)* Well, everything, actually. He's God!
B:	*(Slyly)* But what do you think will happen if you do?
A:	We will die.
B:	No you won't. He'sss pulling your leg. *(A looks at leg)* That tree has the power to let you know the difference between right and wrong. If you eat that fruit, you will be asss wissse asss God.
A:	Really?
B:	Yes. You can trussst me, I'm a sssnake. Take a fruit!

A reaches up, then changes her mind.

A:	Oh, I can't!
B:	Go on!
A:	*(Reaches up again and changes her mind)* No, I can't…
B:	*(Slightly annoyed)* Yesss, you can—go on!
A:	OK…

A reaches up and mimes picking a fruit, then looks really guilty.

B:	Go on, take a bite.
A:	No, I want to put it back.
B:	Ha, too late! You can't put it back! In for a penny, in for a pound. You may asss well take a bite!
A:	N-n-n-no…
B:	You know you want to.
A:	Well, yes, I do, actually. I don't suppose one little bite will do any harm.
B:	*(Whispers an aside)* No, it will jussst lead to the downfall of every ssssingle human being, that'sss all!
A:	What was that?
B:	Oh, nothing important! Jussst take that bite.

A mimes taking a bite and chewing.

Narrator:	Fancy listening to a snake rather than to God. After she had tasted the fruit, Eve gave some to Adam and, after they had both eaten the fruit, they felt very ashamed. They had never felt like this before and they were so frightened that they hid behind some trees. God was very sad because Adam and Eve had disobeyed him. He still loved them but he could no longer trust them. God's caretakers had become *careless* takers and it wasn't long before they started to blame each other for the situation they were in.
A:	Now Adam's blaming me, but it wasn't my fault. It was that snake!
Narrator:	Poor Eve, she made the wrong choice. But God didn't make us like robots, unable to make our own decisions. He made us with independent minds. He wants us to be his friends—not by controlling us but by giving us the free will to choose to be his friends too. After Adam and Eve had disobeyed God, things went from bad to worse—in fact, much worse. Adam and Eve had two sons called Cain and Abel and, when they grew up, Cain killed his brother. Eventually, things got so bad that God finally decided to… *(Pause)* ah, but that's another story. *(Pause)* Come on, you two, time to leave the garden…

All exit.

Day Four: Enough's enough!

Bible story: Genesis 6:1—9:17

Cast
Narrator and two others (A and B)

Props
Thunderstorm sound effects CD, CD player (both optional)

Narrator:	Have you ever been woken up in the morning by a noisy neighbour hammering on the wall? It's a very unpleasant experience.
A:	What are they building now?
B:	Yeah, waking us up like this! They have no consideration at all,
Narrator:	Well, there would have been a lot of sawing and hammering, and *(shouts)* 'timber!'

 Reproduced with permission from *Razzamatazz Robots Holiday Club!* published by BRF 2008 (978 1 84101 577 4)

A mimes hammering and makes a banging noise, while B puts fingers in his/her ears.

Narrator: Yes, there's a lot of noise in today's story.

A carries on making a noise.

Narrator: You see, after Adam and Eve disobeyed God, things went from bad to worse. *(Looks across to A and shouts)* Be quiet!

A: Oops, sorry!

B keeps fingers in his/her ears, not realizing A has stopped.

Narrator: It wasn't just Adam and Eve who disobeyed God. Guess what? So did their children. In fact, one son actually murdered his brother and it didn't stop there. Soon the world was filled with people who were…

A: *(Interrupting and half shouting)* Evil… greedy… selfish… violent… full of hate… angry… it was bad; it was very, very bad!

Narrator: *(Looking across at A)* Er, yes, thank you! Exactly right! Nobody bothered with God any more. No one wanted to be his friend. Enough was enough. God was very sorry that he had made human beings and he said, 'I'll destroy every living creature on earth. I'll wipe out people, animals, birds and reptiles. I'm sorry I ever made them.'

B: *(Takes fingers out of ears)* Actually, that's not right.

Narrator: Oh, so you were listening after all. But, oh yes, it is!

B: Oh no, it isn't! They weren't all…

A: *(Interrupting and half shouting)* Evil… greedy… selfish… violent… full of hate… angry… it was bad; it was very, very bad!

B: Er, yes, thank you, exactly right! Don't forget Noah! Noah was…

A: *(Interrupting)* Evil… Oops, I mean… *(Speaks gently)* kind… generous… gentle… Noah loved and obeyed God.

B: *(Nodding vigorously)* Exactly! And God had noticed Noah and chose not to destroy him or his family. God also loved the animals he had created and decided to save two of every kind of living creature.

Narrator: *(Looking at B in amazement)* Yes, thank you, I was about to get to that part. *(Looks at audience)* So God told Noah to build a boat—in fact, a big boat, a very big boat, called an ark. God told Noah of his plan to flood the world but to save Noah and his family and two of every living creature. And Noah did everything that the Lord told him to do.

A: Cor, I wish I'd been there when Noah had to explain that to his wife. *(Speaking in a high voice)* 'What? Build a huge boat on my lawn? Then it will rain for 40 days? I'll never get the washing dry. And we're going to be living in an ark with all those *(holds nose)* smelly animals?'

Narrator: Er, yes. When we obey God, he promises to save us—but he doesn't promise to make things easy.

B: I expect Noah soon got a bit of a reputation with the neighbours, too. *(Mimes nosey neighbours)* 'Look, here comes noisy Noah. What was that, Noisy Noah? God's going to send a flood and destroy the world? So you're building a huge arky thingy to save you and all the animals? How many storeys high did you say? *(Pause)* Well, it seems like a tall story to me! Ha, ha! Whatever, but no thanks, I won't join you. Mad! Quite mad!'

A: *(Joins in)* Oh, and here come a couple of elephants with their trunks packed and ready, waiting to join noisy Noah in his outsized ark!

Narrator: Yes, well, I'm sure people must have been very rude to Noah and probably made life hard for him, but he was faithful to God and carried on building the ark until finally it was finished.

Thunderstorm sound effects played from a CD. Alternatively, encourage the audience to create the noise of a thunderstorm.

B: It rained and it rained and it rained.

Narrator: God shut the door of the ark. Noah, his family and all the animals were safe inside. The water rose…

A: *(Interrupting and slowly lifting hands)* … higher and higher.

B: Higher than the houses…

A: … and higher and higher.

B: Higher than the trees…

A: … and higher and higher.

B: Higher than the mountains.

Narrator: The earth was finally flooded. It rained for 40 days and 40 nights.

A: Then, when the rain had finally stopped, Noah opened a window and let a raven out, but the bird kept flying and never returned to the ark.

B: Several days later, Noah let out a dove, which finally returned to him with a green olive leaf in its beak. Yes, the water was almost gone. Yippee!

Narrator:	Finally, Noah, his family and the animals all came out of the ark and—first things first—they praised God.

A and B look up at the sky.

B:	Wow! What's that?
A:	A rainbow!
B:	A beautiful, colourful rainbow.
Narrator:	God sent a rainbow as a sign of his promise never to destroy the world again. Whenever you see a rainbow in the sky, it is a reminder of God's promise and the fact that…
All:	God loves you!

Day Five: The Master's plan

Bible story: Luke 2:1–7; John 1:1–5 and 14; Mark 1:1–11; Colossians 1:15–20

Cast
Narrator and two others (A and B)

Props
PowerPoint presentation of the *God's master plan* outline on page 62 (which can be downloaded free from www.barnabasinchurches.org.uk/razzamatazz) or a whiteboard and marker pen.

Narrator:	Noah's children had children, and their children had children, and their children had children, and so on and so on down the generations.
A:	And guess what? We messed up again and again and again.
B:	But God knew we would, and he had a master plan.
Narrator:	It's a bit like this…

Narrator draws the 'God's master plan' presentation outline on a whiteboard. Better still, use PowerPoint, with A and B building each stage as the Narrator talks through the script.

Narrator:	God didn't build us to be robots. He created us with the freedom to make our own choices. It was God's intention that we should be his friends, but for this to happen we need to be as perfect as he is…

A and B either show the PowerPoint image of the world and the heart, or draw the image on the whiteboard.

Narrator:	Unfortunately, it is really difficult for human beings to be perfect. We are for ever thinking, saying and doing things that break the pathway between us and God.

A and B either show the PowerPoint image of the broken pathway or draw the image on the whiteboard.

Narrator:	The broken pathway stops us from loving God, but it doesn't stop God from loving us: God still loves us.

A and B either show the PowerPoint of the 'God still loves us' image or draw the image on the whiteboard.

Narrator:	Two thousand years ago, God's only Son, Jesus, came in person to show us what God is like. Jesus lived the perfect life. He showed us what God is like in everything he said and did, and, when he died on the cross, Jesus paid the price for all the wrong things we have ever said, thought or done. He mended the pathway between God and us.

A and B either show the PowerPoint image of the mended pathway or draw the image on the whiteboard.

Narrator:	We now have the choice to walk along that pathway and say 'thank you' to God or to carry on ignoring his love for us. If we choose to say 'thank you' to God, he wants us to try to live our lives in a way that will please him—but he knows that we can't always help getting in a mess, so he will continue to forgive us when we get things wrong.
A:	This is God's master plan for our lives.
Narrator:	Yes, ever since the very beginning of time, God has longed for us to be his friends.
B:	And thanks to Jesus, we can choose to say 'yes' to God.
All:	YES!

Follow this talk with the 'Razzamatazz rap' on page 22. A recording of the rap, together with all the Razzamatazz Robots songs, is available from John Hardwick's website: www.johnhardwick.org.uk.

God's master plan

Presentation outline

Day One: Creation appreciation!

Can you spot ten differences between the two pictures?

Colour in today's Bible verse.

God looked at what he had done... and it was very good!

Genesis 1:31

Day One: Creation appreciation!

Draw your favourite day of creation from the list below.

1. Light
2. Sky
3. Sea, land, trees and plants
4. Sun, moon and stars
5. Fish and birds
6. Animals and people
7. God rested

Find the words in the grid.

B	I	R	D	S	S	B	X	S	D
E	E	D	A	E	O	Y	T	N	L
A	J	O	H	V	L	F	H	A	R
F	U	L	D	E	Y	I	E	M	O
T	P	L	A	N	T	S	G	U	W
E	Z	N	Y	N	W	H	O	H	A
R	A	T	S	P	D	O	D	L	T
A	N	I	M	A	L	S	R	S	E
H	A	M	A	Z	I	N	G	D	R
F	A	D	E	T	A	E	R	C	J

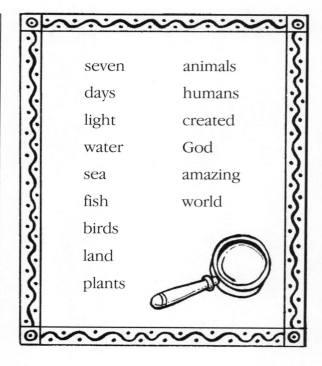

seven animals

days   humans

light   created

water   God

sea   amazing

fish   world

birds

land

plants

Day Two: Creation's crown!

Add colour to the garden for Adam and Eve.

Find your way through the Razzamatazz Robot maze.

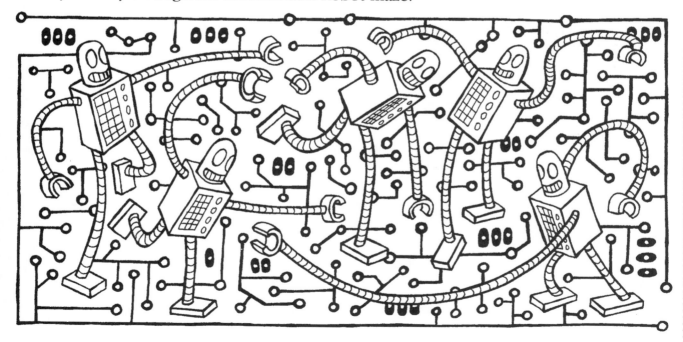

Day Two: Creation's crown!

Put the words of today's memory verse in the correct order—and then see if you can memorize it.

I because you praise will wonderful created of me the 139 you 14 way Psalm

___ _____ _____ _____ _____

____ ____ _____ _____

_____ _____ ____ _____

_____ : _____

You are carefully designed, very special and loved by God. No one is the same as you. But which of the robots below is different from all the rest?

Day Three: Careless whispers!

Play a game of snakes and ladders with a friend. Cut out the spinner and counters to play the game (see page 82). Push a small coloured pencil through the centre of the spinner. If you land on a snake, you have to slide down to the square at its tail. If you land on a ladder, you can climb to the square at the top of the rungs.

Enjoy the Sunshine. Go Forward 3	Have a nap. Lose a turn	Take a bite from the forbidden fruit. Go back to the start.	24.	Finish! 25.
20.	19.	18.	Sit by a stream. Go Forward 2	16.
11.	12.	13.	See a Butterfly. Go Forward 4	15.
Stroke a deer. Go Forward 1	9.	Talk to a bird. Go Forward 3	7.	6.
Start 1.	2.	3.	Take a walk. Go Forward 2	5.

Day Three: Careless whispers!

Break the code to work out today's Bible verse.
Some of the letters have been left in place to start you off.

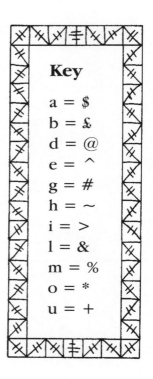

Key

a = $
b = £
d = @
e = ^
g = #
h = ~
i = >
l = &
m = %
o = *
u = +

R _ _ _ _ _ _ r _ t _ _ _ _ _ r _
  ^ % ^ % £ ^   ~ ^ & * @

_ n _ _ _ _ t _ n s , n _
> $ & &   ~ > n # s $ @

_ _ w _ _ s w y _
~ ^   > & &   ~ *   * +

t _ _ r _ _ t w y t _
   ~ ^   > # ~ $ *

_ _ . (P r _ v _ r s 3:6)
*   * ^ £

How many pieces of fruit can you find in the picture below?

Day Four: Enough's enough!

Colour in the picture of Noah and the animals.

Help the rabbits find their way into the ark.

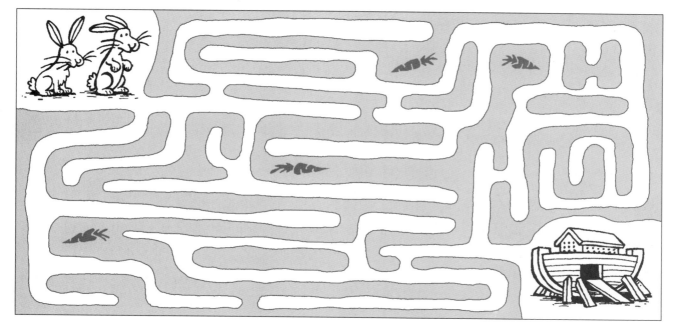

Day Four: Enough's enough!

Draw a picture of your favourite animals going into the ark.

Find the key words of today's Bible memory verse in the wordsearch.

_____ _____ _____ _____ the _____ _____ _____ _____ your _____ _____ _____ with all your
_____ _____ _____ _____ _____ , with all your _____ _____ _____ _____ , with all your
_____ _____ _____ _____ _____ _____ , with all your _____ _____ _____ and love your
_____ _____ _____ _____ _____ _____ _____ _____ as _____ _____ _____ _____ _____ _____ _____ _____ .

Luke 10:27

love   heart
Lord   soul
God   strength
            mind
            neighbour
            yourself

L	O	U	P	T	N	N	E	D
J	O	Q	U	O	E	B	Y	R
U	T	V	F	M	I	N	D	O
S	T	R	E	N	G	T	H	L
D	O	R	L	B	H	P	A	U
V	E	U	S	Y	B	J	E	S
O	G	H	L	G	O	D	O	J
H	E	A	R	T	U	Z	L	K
W	F	L	E	S	R	U	O	Y

Day Five: The Master's plan

Colour the picture of God's master plan. Put yourself in the picture.

God loves us and wants us to be his friends!

We can be on God's side

God still loves us

God's love goes on and on!

Day Five: The Master's plan

Fill in today's Bible memory verse in the grid.

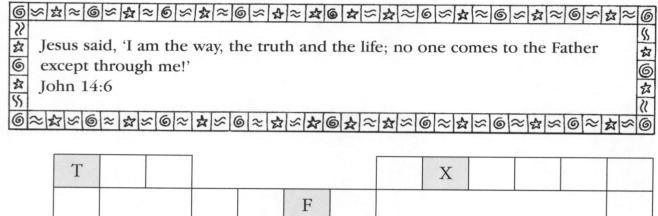

Jesus said, 'I am the way, the truth and the life; no one comes to the Father except through me!'
John 14:6

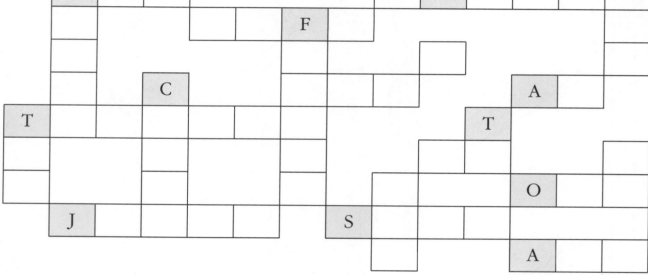

Try performing the Razzamatazz rap with a friend, or as a group.

Jesus came to show the way
Of the Master's plan for us today.
We're not robots, we have the choice
To turn away or follow God's voice!

Jesus died, the price to pay,
But he rose again on Easter Day.
He opens the door and welcomes us in,
He died for us and forgave our sin.

Now God invites you and me
To be a part of his great family!
The Master's plan for us will be
Final destination: heaven's party!

Appendix One

Razzamatazz Robot visors

Creation appreciation! Open your eyes and see the wonder of God's creation. These cool specs help us to stay focused! Cut around the solid lines, then cover the cut-out space with cellophane (available from www.ss-services.co.uk).

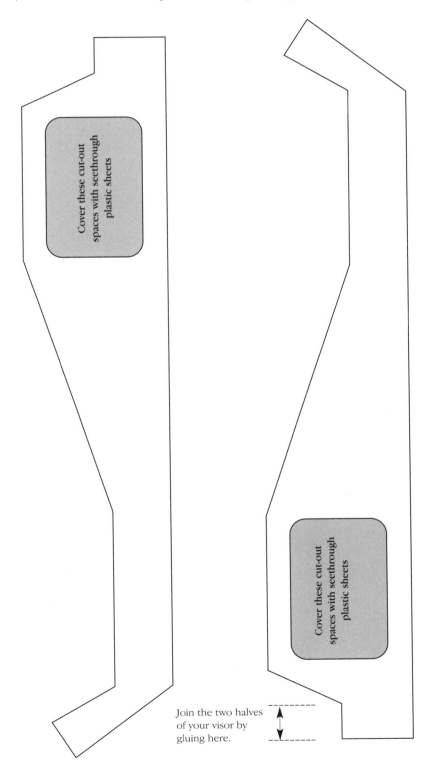

Cover these cut-out spaces with seethrough plastic sheets

Cover these cut-out spaces with seethrough plastic sheets

Join the two halves of your visor by gluing here.

Razzamatazz heart shades

Cut around the solid lines, then cover the cut-out space with cellophane (available from www.ss-services.co.uk).

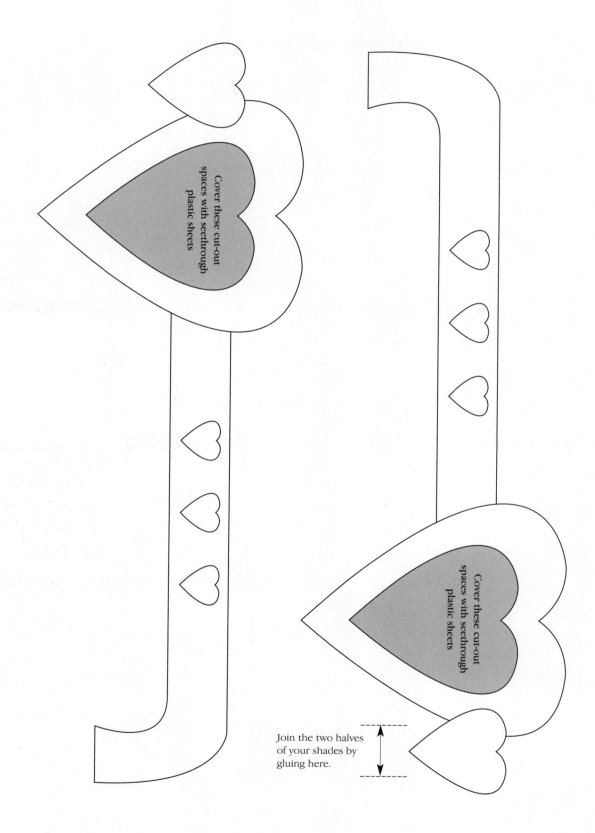

Cover these cut-out spaces with seethrough plastic sheets

Cover these cut-out spaces with seethrough plastic sheets

Join the two halves of your shades by gluing here.

Razzamatazz Robots board game

Colour your robot, cut it out, and then race round the course. Flip a coin to move your robot: heads = 2; tails = 1
Where is your robot race taking place? Is it going through a desert, through mountains, through a city, or across the sea?
Add your own pictures.

Box robot

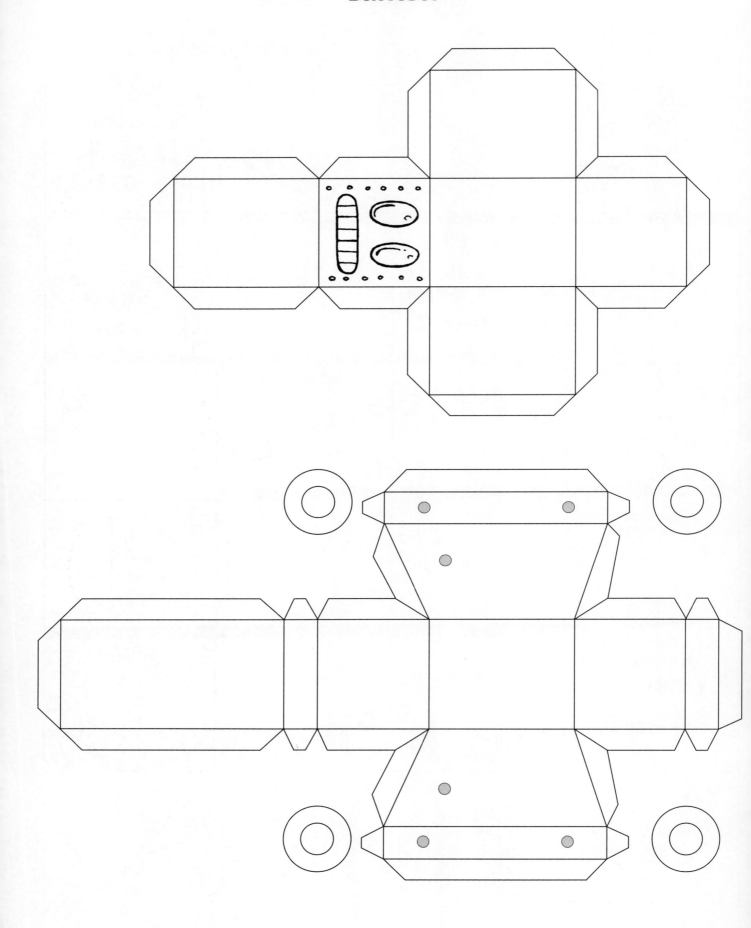

Robot masks

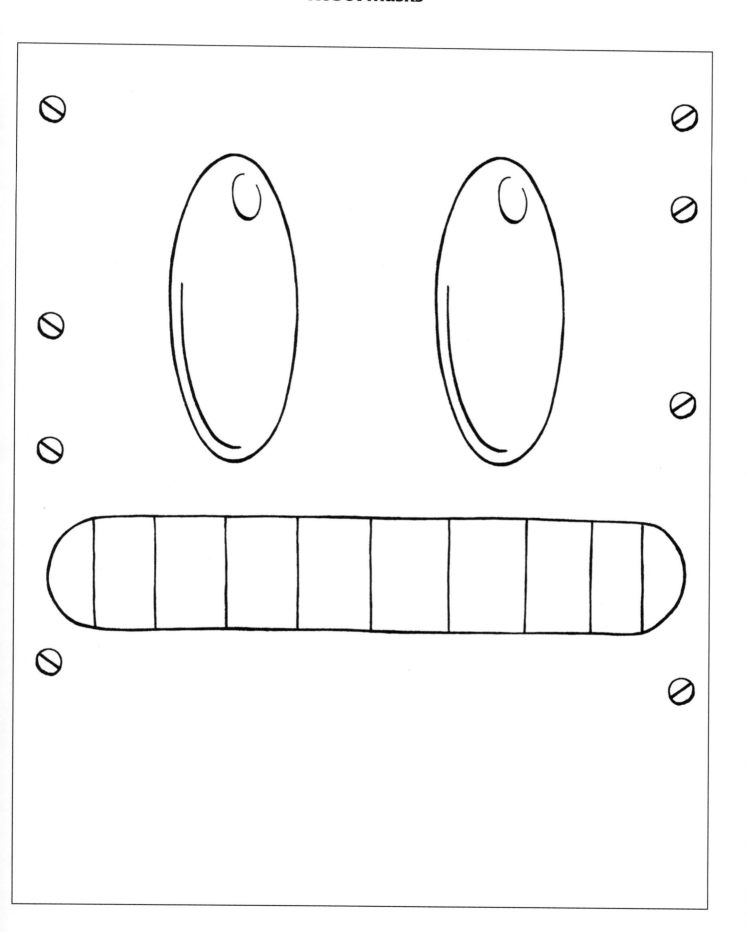

Rainbow headbands

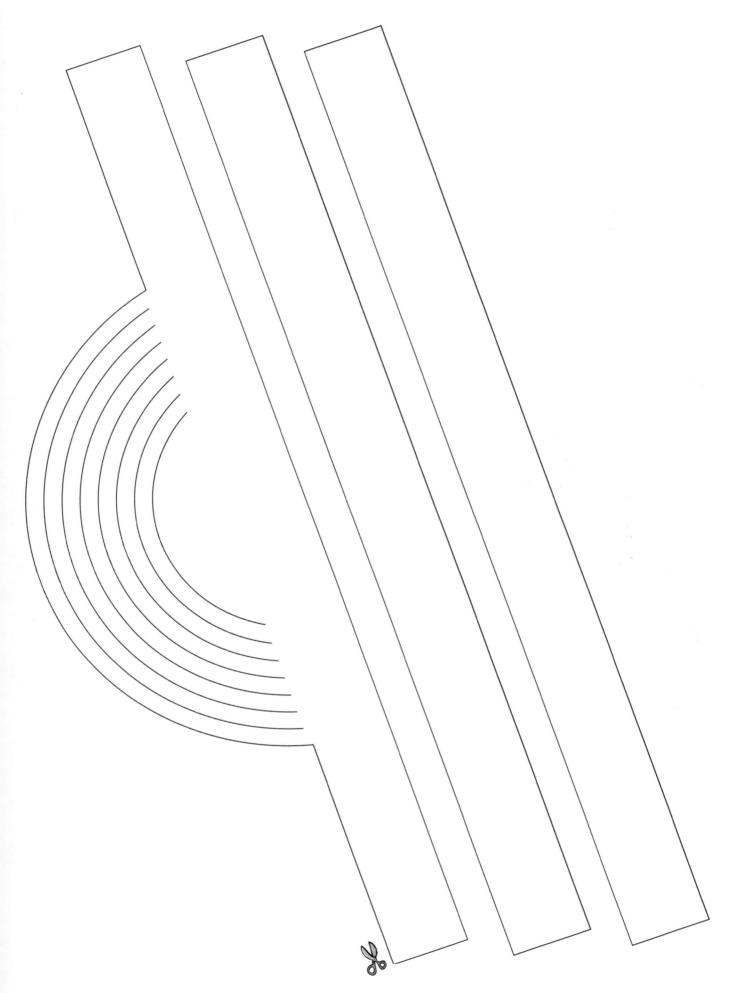

Razzamatazz calendar

God's love goes on and on!

Stick your calendar pad here

Prayer chooser

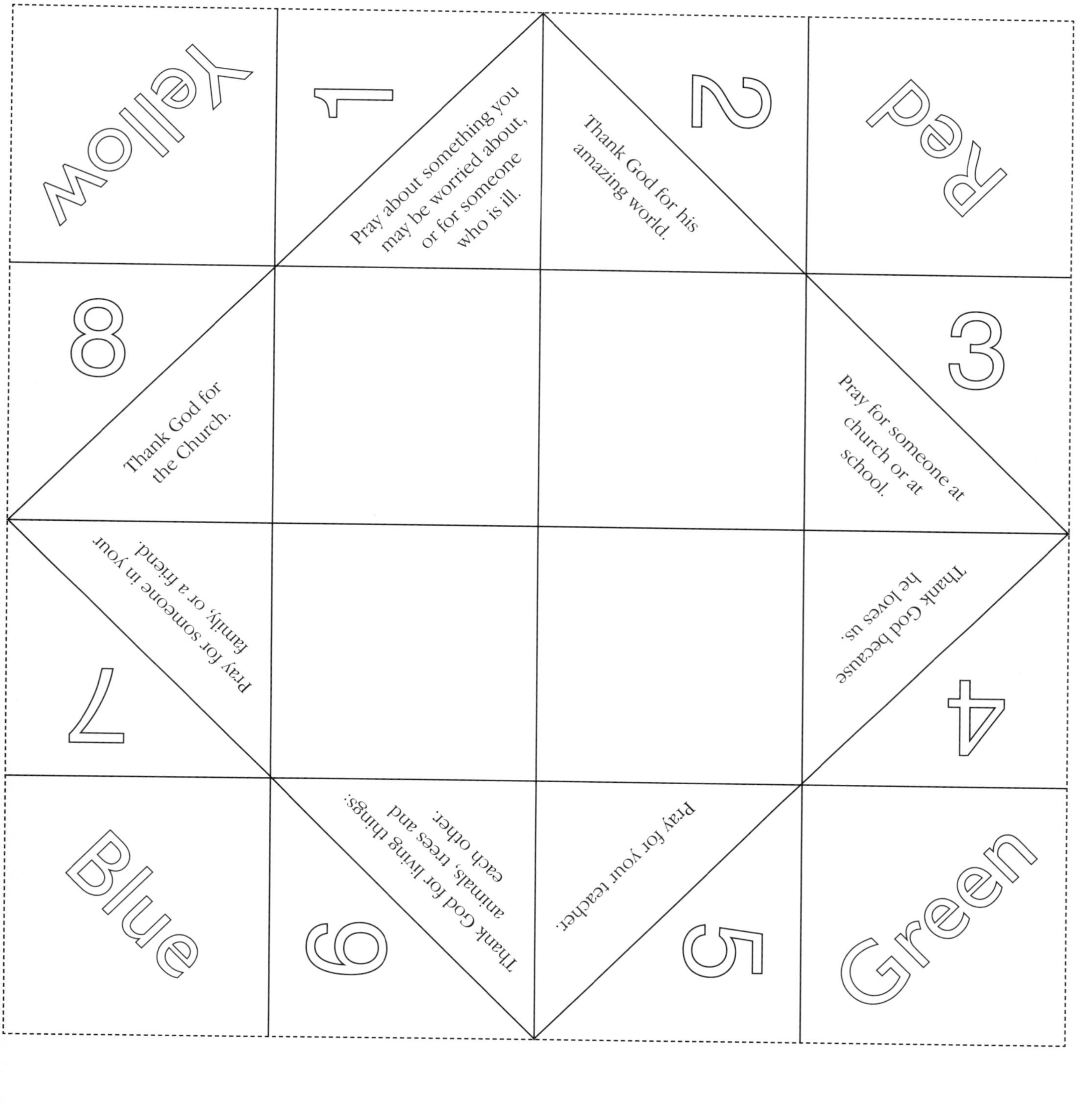

Yellow

1

Pray about something you may be worried about, or for someone who is ill.

Thank God for his amazing world.

2

Red

8

Thank God for the Church.

Pray for someone at church or at school.

3

Pray for someone in your family, or a friend.

Thank God because he loves us.

4

7

Thank God for living things: animals, trees and each other.

Pray for your teacher.

Blue

6

5

Green

 Reproduced with permission from *Razzamatazz Robots Holiday Club!* published by BRF 2008 (978 1 84101 577 4)

Careless whispers!

Spinner and counters

Photocopy spinner and counters on to medium-weight card, so that there are enough for each child, pair of children or small group. The children could colour their spinner and counters before cutting them out and playing the game.

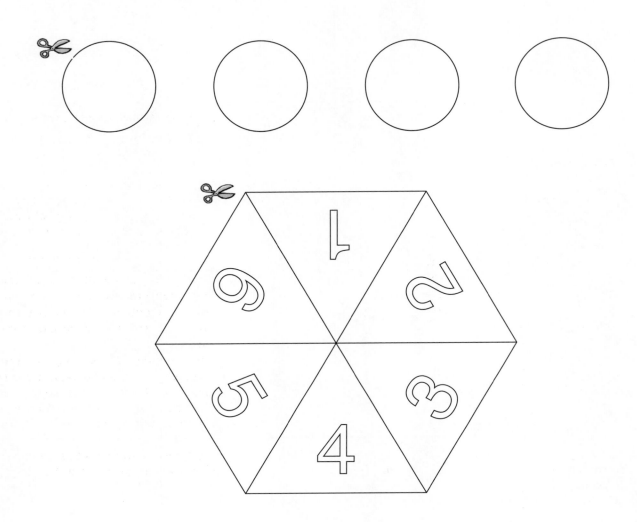

Appendix Two

Material for a special service or evening event

The following pages contain extra ingredients for a special holiday club Sunday service or evening event. Don't forget to include some of the songs and Bible memory verses that the children have learnt, but please remember to add all the songs used during the holiday club on to your Christian Copyright Licence (CCL) list.

Razzamatazz Robots march

Announce that there will be a special Razzamatazz Robots march when the children will wear the craft items they have made during the week. Make sure that the children are well informed about this event in advance so that they remember to come along with their craft items.

Sing the *Razzamatazz Robots* theme song together to set the scene, then play some robotic music as the children march on to the stage to demonstrate the craft items they have made in their holiday club—for example, their Razzamatazz visors or glasses, their robot headbands, and their robot arm and leg bands.

As they march, the children should move like robots in time to the robotic music. When all the children are on stage (or at the front), lead a robotics keep-fit session—for example, star jumps, scissor jumps, press-ups, running on the spot, touching their toes, skipping with an imaginary rope and doing side-stretches.

After the robotics keep-fit, invite the congregation or audience to pretend that they each have a remote control unit with which to control the children. Tell them that if they press number 1, the children will switch off the television and stand to attention, waiting for the next command. If they press number 2, the children will clean their bedrooms. If they press number 3, the children will cook dinner. Have a practice run, with the children miming the commands when you call out the numbers.

Point out to the congregation or audience that, although this sounds idyllic, it wouldn't really be much fun if children only ever did as they were told and only responded to commands. This is how robots operate. But a robot is not alive; it doesn't have a personality and it could never give and receive love in the way that a child does. A robot is just a machine. Finish by saying that we should not take each other for granted: we should remember that God gives us the gift of life and the gift of each other. We are not machines; we are living, breathing, loving human beings, created in the image of God.

Bible memory verse one

Sing the Bible memory verse for Day One (see page 16).

Junk robots judging competition

> **You will need:**
> The junk robots you made during the holiday club, and first, second and third prize rosettes in different colours. (These can be made from some cardboard plates, coloured in and with ribbon attached)

Before the start of the event, move all the junk robots that the teams have made to the front of the church or worship space. Ask a representative from each team to introduce their team's robot, giving its name and showing off its special features.

Invite three or four members of the congregation or audience to form a judging panel and choose a winning robot, plus two runners-up. Point out that we are really all winners, because each robot has been individually created and built by human beings—each one of whom is, of course, unique.

When the judging is over, move the robots to one side and introduce some special guests: the Watt family.

The Watt family's wild robot adventure

> **Cast**
> Narrator, Professor Roly Rolo, Grandma Watt, Rick Watt, Wendy Watt, Robot
>
> **Props**
> Remote control unit (for the professor), a packet of Rolos (for Rick), the Watt family theme tune and a CD player (optional)

Play the Watt family theme tune.

Narrator: Grandma, Rick and Wendy designed and built their own robot. Unfortunately, the robot malfunctioned, so they decided to buy a Razzamatazz robot designed and created by the wonderful Professor Roly Rolo. However, the professor has come to realize that, although his robots are amazing, they are not as amazing as human beings.

Enter Professor Rolo.

Prof Rolo: Ha, yes, Professor Roly Rolo, that's me! Whoever created human beings is the greatest creator ever! I'd like to get to know him.

Enter the Watt family.

Wendy: Professor Rolo, is it true that you've just invented yet another robot?

Prof Rolo: As it happens, it is true! I must admit, it is my best invention yet. I'll program my truly amazing robot to come in now…

Professor Rolo presses the remote control. Enter Grandma and Rick. They come running in, chased by a wild robot.

Prof Rolo: *(Shouting to Grandma)* What have you done to my wonderful robot?

Grandma: All I said was that I had a washing machine that looked just like him.

Rick: Yeah, it was Grandma's little joke, but I don't think the robot found it very funny. It's been chasing us for the last half hour.

Grandma: Do something!

Wendy: Use the remote! Shut it down!

Prof Rolo: Good idea!

Professor Rolo presses the remote control and the robot slows down.

Wendy: It's slowed down, but it hasn't stopped.

Prof Rolo: No, I don't want to shut it down completely, I want to figure out what's wrong. I'll control it so that it comes this way.

The robot slowly turns and starts walking towards Professor Rolo and Wendy.

Wendy: Stop! Stop! Professor Rolo, it's coming straight for us!

Prof Rolo: Yes, I'm trying to control it, but it's overriding my commands. It's out of control.

Wendy: It's speeding up. Run!

The robot chases the Watt family and Professor Rolo around in a big circle.

Rick: It's no good, we'll have to switch it down manually. Use your walking stick, Grandma.

Grandma: I am—I couldn't run this quickly without it.

Rick: No, no—I mean use your stick to trip it up.

Prof Rolo: No, no, no, don't damage it!

Rick: There's no other way, Professor!

Grandma uses her walking stick to trip the robot up. The Watt family all jump on the robot. The robot struggles but finally they manage to switch it off. Professor Rolo watches, looking devastated.

Wendy: Wow, that was a wild robot!

Grandma: Yes, let's dismantle it and take it to the scrap yard.

Prof Rolo: *(Shouts)* No!

Grandma: Why not? It's only scrap metal.

Prof Rolo: It may be only scrap metal to you, but I have spent years developing this robot.

Rick: Here, Professor, you're really upset. Have a Rolo.

Rick offers the Professor a Rolo, but Wendy takes it instead.

Wendy: Mmmm, lovely, thanks, Rick. Now listen, Professor, if you get this upset over a wild and out-of-control robot that isn't actually alive, no wonder God gets upset with us when we choose to turn away from him.

Grandma: Or upset when he sees us destroying his beautiful world.

Rick: Yeah, because the world is the coolest thing God ever made.

Prof Rolo: Not quite, Rick. Human beings are the crown of God's creation. People are fantastic. They are much better than robots because they can make choices for themselves.

Rick: Well said, Professor, have a Rolo…

Prof Rolo: *(Taking a Rolo)* Why, thank you, Rick, how kind!

Grandma: And the most important choice we will ever make is to choose to follow God—following the Maker's instructions.

Rick:	Well said, Grandma, have a Rolo…
Grandma:	*(Taking a Rolo)* Why, thank you, Rick, how kind!
Narrator:	Well, all's well that ends well—or perhaps that's another story! Anyway, that's the end of the Watt family's robotic adventure, but I'm sure there'll be many more adventures to come, so do join us again!

Play the Watt family theme tune. Rick and Wendy pull the wild robot to his feet and help him as everyone exits, waving as they go.

Bible memory verse two

Sing the Bible memory verse for Day Two (see page 17).

Bible story summary

> **Cast**
> Narrator and two others (A and B)

| Narrator: | You know, when we look at some of the amazing machines and incredible robots that have been invented, we may feel a bit small and not very important or clever. But God loves each one of us, however small we are. Jesus told a story about something that didn't seem very special—but someone thought it was. And this something had got lost. |

Enter A, searching for something.

Narrator:	*(To A)* What have you lost?
A:	Something very, very important.
Narrator:	What, car keys?
A:	Nope!
Narrator:	Credit card?
A:	Nope!
Narrator:	What, then?
A:	A sheep—and I've got to find him.
Narrator:	What, now? But it's dark and cold outside, and there are lots of wild animals.

A exits stage left. B wanders on from stage right, looking shy.

Narrator:	*(To B)* You're looking rather sheepish.
B:	That's because I'm pretending to be a sheep—in fact, a lost sheep.
Narrator:	You should be on all fours, then.
B:	No, I'm a clever sheep. I've learnt to walk upright. Right?
Narrator:	Oh? OK, then. So how did you get lost? Did you plan it? *(In a sheep's voice)* 'Toda-a-ay's the da-a-ay I esca-a-ape and run awa-a-ay' *(In a normal voice)* How do you reckon the sheep got lost?
B:	I reckon the sheep was eating some grass, then looked up and noticed some even greener grass, so wandered across. Then it looked up and saw some more, then some more, and more, and more, and more… until eventually it wandered further and further away from the shepherd and out of sight. It was lost and scared and alone. Anyway, I think I'll carry on wandering and try to find my way home, so excuse me.

B wanders off, stage right. A comes back on, stage left.

| A: | Oh she-e-ep, where are you? Oh, it's no good, I've searched high and I've searched low. Perhaps he's been eaten by a wild animal and all I'll find are lamb chops. But he may be alive; I can't give up. |

A wanders off stage again. B wanders on and then wanders off. Both keep missing each other, until eventually they spot each other from either side of the stage. They run towards each other in slow motion, arms outstretched. B picks up A and puts him on his shoulder.

A:	Here, put me down. *You're* the sheep. I'm meant to put you on *my* shoulder.
B:	Oh yes, I forgot… *(They swap)*
Narrator:	So the shepherd finally got his sheep home. I wonder what he said when his lost sheep was safely back in the sheepfold.
A:	You stupid sheep! If you try to run off like that again, I'll wrap you up in cotton wool!
Narrator:	No, that's not what he said! He said he was so happy to have found his sheep that he would call all his friends round

for a party. *(To B, who has started wandering again)* Don't start wandering off again! It's so easy to do.

B: Yes, It's easy to wander away from God and get lost. But God loves us so much that he comes to find us and leads us back home.

A: Yes, Jesus came to rescue us, just like the shepherd rescued the sheep.

Narrator: Jesus is the good shepherd and his love goes on and on and on.

A and B: So don't wander off!

Bible memory verse

For God so loved the world

Sing the extra day's Bible memory verse song (see page 21). This song can also be found on *Action Packed Praise 1* DVD and CD by John Hardwick.

Prayer activity

Start by reminding everyone that we can pray to God anytime and anywhere. If we wish, we can close our eyes so that we don't get distracted by things going on around us. When we say 'Amen' it shows that we have finished praying or that we agree with someone else's prayer. Go on to say that we can pray at home, at school, at church—anywhere. We can pray in our bedrooms on our own or as part of a big crowd at church; we can pray while walking the dog or riding a bike (but don't close your eyes if you're riding a bike!). It's a real privilege to pray to God, so let's pray!

Hold up a teaspoon and explain that in cookery books we often see the word 'teaspoon' abbreviated to TSP. This abbreviation is a helpful way for us to think about what to say when we pray to God. First of all, we can say 'Thank you' to God… next we can say 'Sorry' to God… and, finally, we can say 'Please'. For example:

'Thank you for our friends and family; thank you for Jesus, our closest friend; thank you that each one of us is special to you and for loving us so much.'

'Sorry for the times when we have got things wrong; for the times when we turned away from you and gone our own way; for the hurtful things we have said to others and for the things we have thought that have made you sad.'

'Please help us to be more like Jesus in all we think, say and do; help us to live our lives for you and to put you above all other things. Please help our friends and those we love, especially when they are unwell or going through difficult times.'

Appendix Three

Razzamatazz Robots! badges

Use the templates below to make badges for the children. Photocopy on to thin card and attach a safety pin to the back with a strip of masking tape. The children can colour in their own badges and write their names in the space. Younger children might need team leaders to help them write their names.

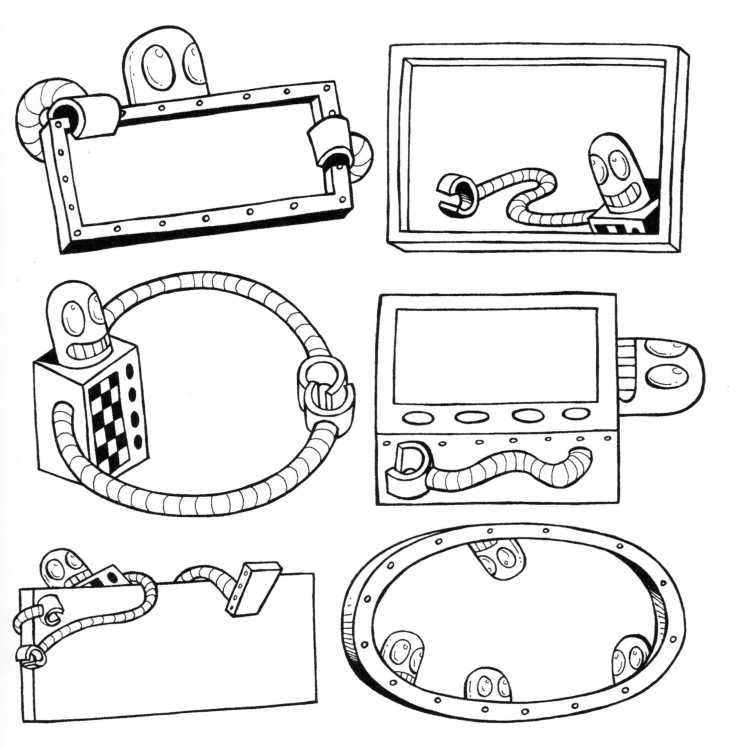

Razzamatazz Robots! invitation cards

Photocopy the template below to make invitation cards for your *Razzamatazz Robots!* holiday club. The children can colour them in and give them out to their friends and classmates.

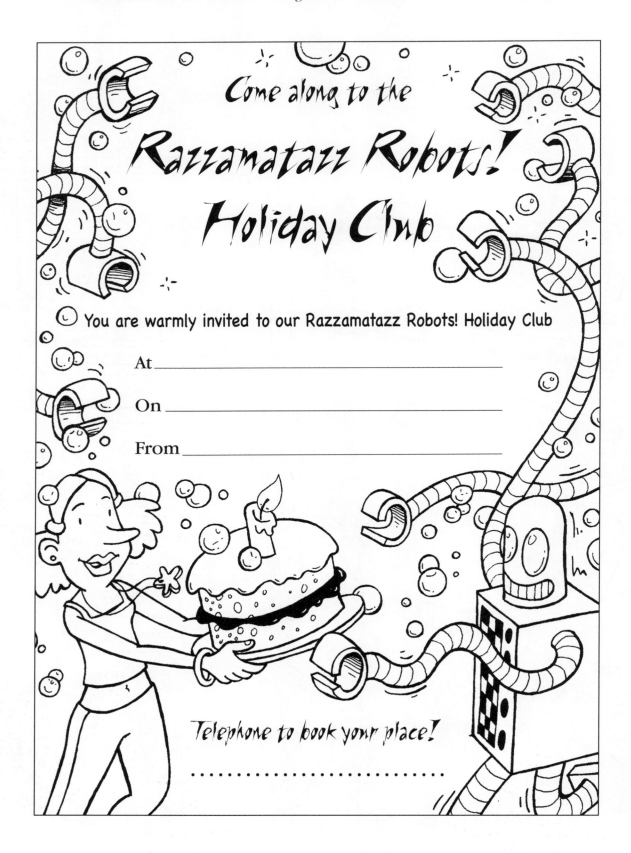

Razzamatazz Robots! registration form

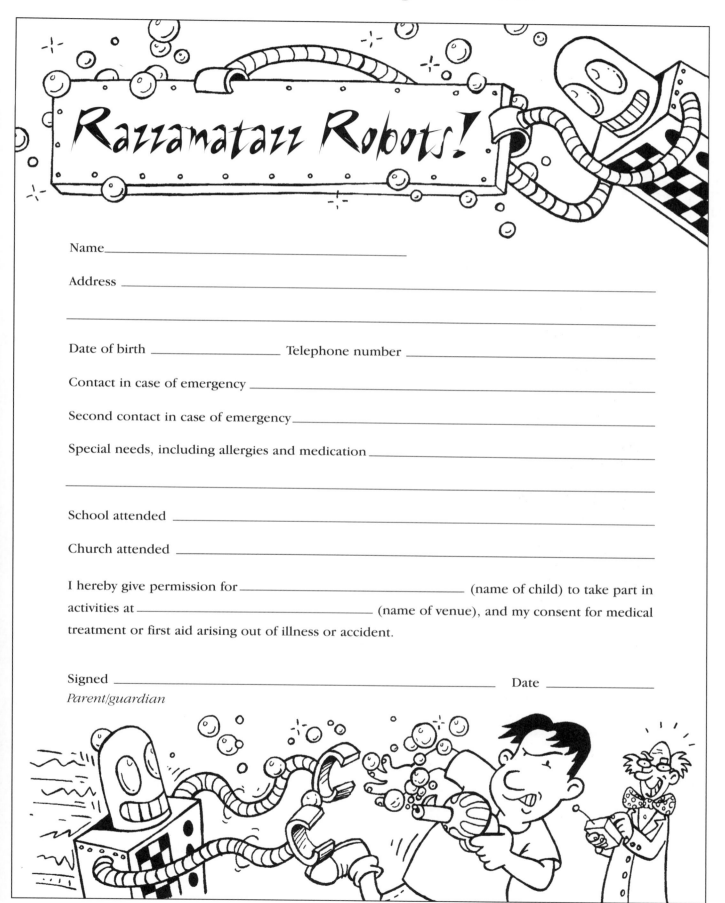

Name_____

Address _____

_____

Date of birth _____ Telephone number _____

Contact in case of emergency _____

Second contact in case of emergency_____

Special needs, including allergies and medication _____

_____

School attended _____

Church attended _____

I hereby give permission for _____ (name of child) to take part in

activities at _____ (name of venue), and my consent for medical

treatment or first aid arising out of illness or accident.

Signed _____ Date _____

Parent/guardian

Razzamatazz Robots! presentation poster

Use this poster to invite parents, relatives and friends to a *Razzamatazz Robots!* event
to find out what the children have been doing during their holiday club week.

Appendix Four

Time fillers, speedy games and prayer ideas

Time fillers

Design a logo

You might like to think about designing a logo for your team, or an overall logo for your *Razzamatazz Robots!* holiday club.

Design a Razzamatazz robot

Design a Razzamatazz robot for your team. What special features would you give it? Some ideas could include X-ray eyes, solar panels on the head for energy and so on.

Word busters

Give the children sheets of paper with the words 'Razzamatazz Robots' written on the top. They have to see how many words they can make, only using the available letters once in each word and not using plurals or proper nouns.

Extra craft ideas

See page 43 for instructions to make a team junk model robot or a creation collage.

Razzamatazz Robots! bookmark
Photocopy the template on to thin card to make *Razzamatazz Robots!* bookmarks (see page 92). The children can colour in their bookmark, write their name in the space and keep the bookmark as a souvenir of their holiday club fun.

Speedy games

Like and don't like

Sit the children in a circle. Give a category, such as a colour, a television programme or a food. Ask the first child to begin by saying their name, followed by one thing they like in the chosen category and one thing they don't like. The next child then does the same, but has to start by saying that they like the thing their neighbour didn't like. (For example, 'I'm John and I like yellow but I don't like pink…'; 'I'm Jane and I like pink, but I don't like red…' and so on.) Play the game as fast as possible. Use different categories until the energy goes out of the game. Alternatively, if a child gets the item their neighbour disliked wrong, then they are out of the game (but stay seated in the circle). The game continues until only one child is left.

Grandma's chips

Ask for a volunteer and interview them. The only answer they are allowed to give to the questions you ask is 'Grandma's chips'. The interview might include questions such as, 'What's your name? What did you have for breakfast? Dinner? Tea? What shampoo do you use? What football team do you support? What do I look like?' To all of these questions the volunteer has to reply 'Grandma's chips' without smiling or laughing.

What am I holding in my hand?

The leader thinks of an item, which could be anything of any size—for example, something in the room, a football team, a pop group, a colour, a musical instrument, something you find in a kitchen, an animal and so on. The leader holds out a closed hand and says, 'What am I holding in my hand?' The children then have to try to guess what the leader is thinking of. The children put their hands up to suggest answers, and whoever guesses correctly gets a small prize (such as a sweet) or a point for their team.

Friends

Choose two friends to be your volunteers. Ask one of the two friends to leave the room and ask the other friend three questions, such as 'What is your friend's least favourite subject at school? What is your friend's favourite pop group?' and so on. When the first volunteer has answered the questions, ask the other to come back into the room. Now ask the second child the same questions and see how well their friend knows them.

Categories

Ask two children to sit down facing each other. Give them a category, such as something you would find in the kitchen, varieties of chocolate bar and so on. Each child takes it in turn to think of something in that category. The one who dries up first or repeats something is out. Choose someone else to take on the champion until you have an overall winner.

Prayer ideas

Prayer tree

A prayer tree fits in with the *Razzamatazz Robots* theme of creation appreciation and the celebration of life. Create a tree out of large sheets of sugar paper, or use a picture of a tree enlarged to an appropriate size, and affix to a wall. You can either have a tree for each team or one large tree for the whole club. If you are feeling really creative, you could make your tree out of thick card and add a base so that it can be free-standing.

For each day, cut different fruit shapes out of card so that the children can write prayers on them and stick them to the tree with sticky tape or Blu-tack. For example, Day One could be apples, Day Two could be grapes, Day Three could be pears and so on. Make sure the children know that their prayers might be read out aloud. At an appropriate time during each day's programme, have a leader read out some of the different prayers on the tree and then lead a group prayer.

Having a different fruit for each day will mean that you know which prayers were written on a particular day. By the end of the holiday club, the prayer tree will be covered in bright fruit—the children's prayers lifted up to God.

This bookmark belongs to:

○ _____

Appendix Five

Further resources and training events

Music

All the songs that accompany the *Razzamatazz Robots!* holiday club are available from John Hardwick's website: www.johnhardwick.org.uk.

Razzamatazz Robots! DVD and CD

Produced by John Hardwick and ACM Studios. See the songs in action and sing along.

The *Razzamatazz Robots!* DVD provides great visual material, recorded especially to complement this book. It's ideal for projecting at holiday clubs and also makes a good prize or present. The DVD includes:

- *Razzamatazz Robots!* Watt family adventure
- *Razzamatazz Robots!* theme song
- *Razzamatazz Robots!* Bible verse songs and backing tracks
- Bonus features: *Razzamatazz* quiz board and Bible stories

Available from: www.johnhardwick.org.uk
www.acm-studio.co.uk/razzrobots.html

You can also check out some of John's songs on YouTube: search for 'John Hardwick'.

Stay legal!

Please remember to tick any songs used during your holiday club or in your weekly church services on your Christian Copyright Licence (CCL) list.

John Hardwick's events

John Hardwick also offers a range of events, including:

- **Training sessions**: A host of ideas with a particular focus on storytelling and music for anyone involved in leading services and events where children are present.
- **Praise parties**: High-energy, fast-moving sessions for primary-aged kids.
- **New songs sessions**: A chance to see John's infectious songs in action.
- **All-age services**: Plenty of variety with a message for everyone.
- **Holiday clubs**: John offers a fun-packed holiday club package including stage-based presentations, songs, Bible narrations and puppetry.
- **Tours**: John tours with a fast-moving presentation. Having the author of the holiday club material coming to your church could be an attractive 'follow-up' event.

For further information about any of the above products or events, please contact John at:

Telephone: 01223 235106
Email: johnhardwick36@hotmail.com
Website: www.johnhardwick.org.uk

It's exciting to hear how my holiday club themes have been used, so please do email me to say how you got on.

Schools work

John is a member of BRF's *Barnabas* team and offers full-day RE presentations bringing the Bible to life through the creative arts, including music, creative storytelling, puppetry and circus skills. A typical day with John might include:

- A 20-minute assembly with the theme 'Working together and valuing one another'. The assembly includes a juggling talk, song and Bible story told in a dramatic way and is suitable for collective worship across Key Stages 1 and 2.

- A 40- to 50-minute assembly with the theme 'Creation appreciation', leading into our uniqueness and how we need to show respect and compassion for others. This is John's most popular theme and could be shortened for younger years. The presentation includes Bible stories told in a dramatic way, a creative poem, a puppet sketch, music and songs, a juggling story with a diabolo, questions and plenty of participation. Ideally, the presentation needs to take place in the school hall or similar space. The material is designed to meet the needs of different year groups across Key Stages 1 and 2 and could be repeated with each year group as required.
- A 30-minute class or year group presentation exploring the value of books and the Bible. This includes a Bible story told in a dramatic way, a puppet sketch, song, juggling, unicycling and other circus skills. Ideally, the presentation needs to take place in the school hall or similar space. The material is designed to meet the needs of different year groups across Key Stages 1 and 2 and will be repeated with each year group as required.
- A 'circus skills' workshop suitable for Years 5 and 6. The workshop offers the opportunity for pupils to try their hand at skills such as juggling, plate-spinning, stunt sticks and diabolos. Maximum number per group: 30 children.

To book John for a *Barnabas RE Day*, or for further details, contact:

BRF, 15 The Chambers, Vineyard, Abingdon OX14 3FE
Telephone: 01865 319700
Fax: 01865 319701
Email: enquiries@brf.org.uk
Website: www.barnabasinchurches.org.uk

Puppet suppliers

Children Worldwide

Full range of puppets and other children's resources.

Children Worldwide Dalesdown
Honeybridge Lane, Dial Post, Horsham RH13 8NX
Telephone: 01403 711032
Website: www.childrenworldwide.co.uk

Hands up for God

People, animal and biblical character puppets plus other related resources and ministry events.

Hands up for God Ministries
34 Holbourne Close, Barrow-upon-Soar
Leicestershire LE12 8NE
Telephone: 01509 415129
E-mail: dennis@handsupforgod.com
Website: www.handsupforgod.com

One Way UK

A full range of puppets.

One Way UK, Unit D1, Acre Business Park, Acre Road
Reading RG2 0SA
Telephone: 0845 490 1929
Email: info@onewayuk.com
Website: www.onewayuk.com

Useful websites

www.barnabasinchurches.org.uk: packed with ideas, resources and news from the *Barnabas* ministry team, plus information about how to book members of the *Barnabas* team for a holiday club, activity day or training event.

www.coloriez.com: a website with pictures to colour.

www.gsuslive.co.uk: a mobile trailer designed for use in school. An interactive and exciting programme aiming to bring RE to life.

www.request.org.uk: witness baptism, visit different styles of churches, see the way they worship and find out what they believe.

www.countiesuk.org: an organization that helps support Christian workers (including John Hardwick) and initiatives across the UK. They also produce 'Wow Factor' Bible exhibitions: Many workers run holiday clubs.

www.childrenworldwide.org.uk: has over 40 children workers across the UK.

www.scriptureunion.org: has over 40 school workers and evangelists across the UK.

★ ★ ★ ★ ★ ★ ★

Holiday club resources

By John Hardwick

978 1 84101 545 3, £8.99

The Starship Discovery Holiday Club! uses the ever-popular theme of outer space to explore another journey: the journey of a life with Jesus himself. Using the example of one of Jesus' closest friends, Peter the fisherman, the material explores five qualities common not just to Peter but also to Christians today. Each day comprises Bible story narration, serial drama/adventure story, puppet sketches, quick quizzes, games and crafts, action songs with music notation, and differentiated fun sheets. Photocopy permission is included.

barnabas

Resourcing people to work with 3–11s

in churches and schools

- Articles, features, ideas
- Training and events
- Books and resources
- www.barnabasinchurches.org.uk

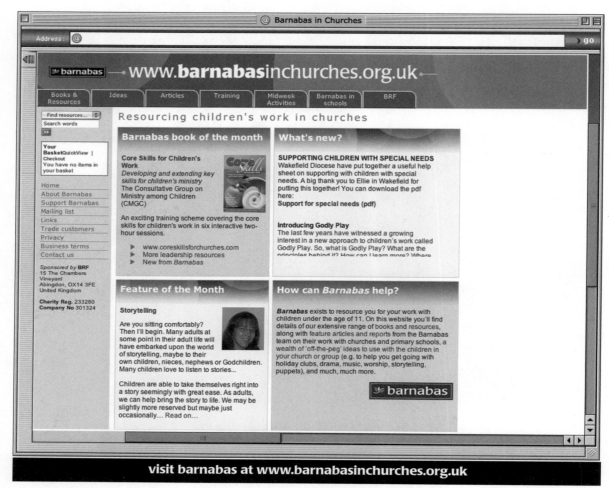

Barnabas is an imprint of brf

BRF is a Registered Charity

Have you signed up to receive the Barnabas monthly email?

To receive mailings about *Barnabas* resources and services, sign up at:

www.barnabasinchurches.org.uk